Rise & Shine

A Conscious Way of Life

You must believe in yourself first.
All else follows.

By
Lois Marie Gacher, CLC
High Esteem Seminars
©2011

Tools to Meet the Challenges of Life

Order this book online at www.trafford.com
or email orders@trafford.com

Most Trafford titles are also available at major online book retailers.

A Note about the Quotes used in this Workbook:

The inclusion of quotes by others is not intended to imply that any of the persons quoted agree with or
endorse any of the ideas or positions of the author. The quotes are intended only as thought provoking
evidence that others have expressed the same ideas throughout the ages of mankind.

Printed in the United States of America.

ISBN: 978-1-4251-4390-9 sc

Trafford rev.   11/29/2011

 www.trafford.com

North America & International
toll-free: 1 888 232 4444 (USA & Canada)
phone: 250 383 6864 ♦ fax: 812 355 4082

Dedicated to
my mother and father
Mary and Louis

Thanks!

To my family:

Phran Gacher and Grace Genise-Redfield, from the beginning their ideas and support over many, many hours made this work possible.

Jean Ervin, for her invaluable editing and ideas that made me stretch, revise, and extend the scope of this book.

Dawn Edwards, and Courtney Genise, for being there, listening, suggesting and supporting whenever I needed it.

To my friends:

Margie Shaffer for her excellent proof reading skills and revising ideas, seeing what I couldn't see.

Judy Prater, bestest friend, for always being there with words of understanding and encouragement.

And a very Special Thanks:

To Brian Altomare of Nuvo-Creative who designed such beautiful graphics for the front and back covers. His work is professional, innovative, and creative. He listens to what you have in mind, and then expands and improves on the concept. A true master at photography, graphics and combining the two for incredible results. When you want the absolute best for designing graphics or a photographer to record those special moments, this is the man to call on. You'll find him at www.nuvo-creative.com. He's the best.

Contents

Part V: _A Wrap Up_

Part VI: Appendix

Rise&Shine

Magic happens when you're not watching...

You are never given a
wish without also being
given the power to make
it true. You may have to
work for it however.
- Richard Bach, *Illusions*

Put your heart, mind, intellect, and soul
even to your smallest acts. This is the
secret of success.
- Swami Sivananda

It takes courage to
grow up and turn
out to be who you
really are.
- e.e. cummings

Chapter 1

The 2nd Secret

Your Inner Matrix

Whationsare you looking for in your life? What is missing that you wish you had? What if you could learn the way to make your dreams a reality? What if you knew exactly what to do and how to do it to have everything you want in your life...to know success? It is within your grasp to have happiness in every possible form, be it health, wealth, or the relationships in your life. Anything you want can be yours when you learn how to work with a seldom understood Universal Law, the Law of Attraction. The first Secret is that with this Law you pull your desires into your life, just like a magnet pulls metal. What you think about, feel strongly about, is attracted to you. Then why don't you have everything you want? Because there is a second Secret – the construct of your inner matrix.

Thoughts generate energy. They *are* energy. This energy goes out in waves from you to affect other vibrations. Like will attract like; whatever you have the strongest feeling towards, the energy of your thoughts will seek out and bring back to you. Positive or negative, it doesn't matter. The kind of energy you are projecting will come back to you in like energy but in a material form. In other words, be warned. Dwelling on negative things is not likely to bring you what you want. As the old Johnny Mercer song goes,

3

The Universe is not punishing you or
blessing you. The Universe is
responding to the vibrational
attitude you are emitting.
- Jerry Hicks,
The Science of Deliberate Creation

If you understand,
things are just as they are;
if you do not understand,
things are just as they are.
- Zen proverb

"You've got to accentuate the positive, eliminate the negative, latch on to the affirmative." Easier said than done.

Perhaps you think that the Law of Attraction might work for some people, but doesn't work for you. You've tried thinking positive and still nothing good happened. Life is just that way for you. You are right. It is that way because *you believe it so*. It is what you think it is because you have created it to be that way with your own thoughts.

The Law of Attraction works with the images in your mind. Your thoughts have manifested things in your life because you have attracted them as like attracts like. A magnetic signal goes out from you and brings back your thoughts in material form. The Law does not distinguish between good and bad. If it is what you are thinking about, then it must be what you want, and so that is what it will bring to you. Any thought generated by strong emotion will continue to project a strong attraction until it is nullified by an opposing thought of equal strength. Negative or positive energy, it works the same.

Whether you believe in it or not, doesn't matter. Like another Universal Law, the Law of Gravity, it is constantly working. It does not require your belief, nor your understanding to work. You cannot turn it off and on when it suits you. It is simply an ongoing process from which you will either benefit or suffer depending on whether or not you know how to use it. Every little thing in your life is a physical manifestation of your thoughts. The energy you have generated with your thoughts and feelings has drawn all the things in your life to you, just like metal to a magnet.

When you think different thoughts, you put out a different energy which will attract to you things in that similar vibration. All energy vibrates at a certain resonance and all things are energy. Quantum physics teaches us that all things are composed of moving particles and nothing is solid. You will simply bring back to you in some material form the same energy that you are sending out. So if you want to change your life, you have to begin with changing your thoughts. How do you do that?

You have about 60,000 thoughts a day. Any one of them that you feel intensely about will generate energy in the direction of that thought. That energy will flow from you to seek out its match in the physical realm and dutifully bring it on back to you.

You are either attracting or repelling in accord with your mental attitudes. You are either identifying yourself with lack or with abundance, with love and friendship or with indifference. You cannot keep from attracting into your experience that which corresponds to the sum total of your states of consciousness.
- Ernest Holmes, *365 Days of Richer Living*

I let go of everything unlike my goal and give attention only to the direction I am taking.
- Alan Cohen, *Handle With Prayer*

Thoughts and feelings are partners. What you are thinking about determines how you feel. How you feel will generate more of the same type thoughts. You are creating your future by the thoughts and feelings of today. Every day you continue to do this. Every day you have a choice. At any time you can choose to terminate a thought that is not doing you any good, change your feelings, and get a different result than you had before.

When you shift your emotions, you are changing your thinking. Your mood and attitude will follow and subsequently so will your life. You are the creator of your life. Each time you think, you create energy which can become something in material form. Be a deliberate creator and create what you want.

The Secret, a book and film by Australian Rhonda Byrne, tells us to think of the Universe as a huge catalog. Pick out what you want. Use the Creative Process to your advantage. *Ask* for what you want. Place your order. Be absolutely certain, perfectly clear, about what it is. Then just like when you place an order with a physical business, believe you will receive it. You ordered it, so it will be delivered. Have certainty it is yours. You've sent a ripple out into the energy field of the Universe, and it will change to accommodate your wishes. If you have a wide open channel, it will come right in. If there are obstacles, it may take a little longer as things are rearranged to clear a path.

The attracting, however, is not the hard part. That is automatic. An unchangeable Law of the Universe. The hard part is attracting exactly what you want without being distracted by negative things you don't want. If you are not attracting what you want, then obviously your thoughts must change. So how do you change them when it is the way you are used to thinking?

You start with Awareness, becoming aware of what you are thinking and feeling and why. Examine the choices you have made in your life and determine why you made them. Once you are aware of your choices and why you made them, you can decide if they truly reflect what you want in your life now. Change the ones that no longer work. Every day you have the opportunity to choose again. Your life will be what you want if you make your choices with awareness. That means being totally clear about what you want, ignoring the manipulations of what others might want for you. If you're really honest with yourself, you'll get what you want.

All life is an experiment. The more experiments you make, the better.
- Ralph Waldo Emerson

When we see choice instead of chance, we become the creator of our experience.
- Alan Cohen, *Joy Is My Compass*

Your choices are based on how you feel about yourself. When you go all the way to the core of your being, your self esteem, and repair any faults in that inner matrix, you will attract to you only that which you want.

Some attractions are stronger than others and therefore last longer. A short intense attraction will bring something to you, but you may not keep it long. Stronger attractions last a lifetime. Look around at everything in your life. Every single item in it, be it a person, animal, thing, job, location, everything you have attracted to you for a purpose. On some level it was what you wanted. Things not there, you simply haven't thought about as strongly. Less thought, less energy, less attraction. It's all about controlling your thoughts to reflect what you want in your life so that you will attract those things to you. Where you live, how you live, and even the type of dwelling you live in is a direct result of your thoughts. You are directly responsible for your environment. You have created it with your thoughts.

Some of your choices can cause not so good experiences. When you experience limitations, it's because of your ignorance of the Law of Attraction. The Universal Law is obedient to your thoughts. You attract what you are thinking about because the Law of Attraction always works.

If there is something you really, really want but you don't get it, then there is something else going on. There's a reason you haven't gotten it: you're repelling it at the same time. Examine the issue from every side. Turn it like a multi-faceted crystal. Search out the smallest thought that might be sending out the message, "Not yet. There's one more thing that must be in place before it can happen." You want *something*. But it can't come through a closed door. What ever you must do to open that door, do it. If you don't have all your ducks in a row, it won't happen. Make space for it in your life. Nature abhors a vacuum.

The Law of Attraction implies that anything is within your field of possibility if you desire it strongly, believe in it, and take action towards it. Besides being crystal clear on what you want, you also must supply action. You must take definite steps to bring about what you desire, even if they're only baby steps. You must want it. You must believe that it is possible for you to have it. And you must expect to get it. If any of these are missing –

The mind is like a drunken monkey,
forever jumping around,
never staying steady.
- Zen saying

Be here now. - Ram Daas

Desire, Belief, Expectation, or if you fail to take the necessary action to make it happen, it won't. If you feel you don't deserve it for any reason, you won't get it. Your inner matrix must be shown you do deserve it. That's where your self esteem comes in.

Essential for success is good self esteem. If you don't have a healthy respect for yourself, how can you possibly attract to you all the good things that you want?

> There is nothing either good or bad,
> but thinking makes it so.
> - William Shakespeare, *Hamlet*

> The only person
> who is with us our entire life,
> is ourselves.

> *The whole search for enlightenment is to seek within,*
> *to become aware that you are complete in yourself.*
> *- Swami Rama*

Chapter 2

Self Esteem

What Is It?

*D*oes someone else's opinion of you determine how you feel about yourself? What determines your value: what you think of yourself or what others think of you? Self esteem is the image you hold of yourself in your mind, how you feel about yourself. It means having an inner security that won't be diminished by turmoil. The stronger your inner security, the less you require approval from others. What makes us all different is what we have in common, the components of self esteem: heredity, instinct, experience. These form your Inner Matrix, that is, what makes you the person you are distinct from every other person on this earth. There is only one you.

Whether you hail from America or Africa, China or Columbia, Paris or Peoria, your self esteem is important. It doesn't matter where you feel you are in the social strata – anywhere from high society to the barrio – your self esteem can still be high or low. Your self esteem determines how you see yourself in life, which opportunities you will choose to experience, and which you will walk away from setting your limitations. The lower your expectations for yourself, the less self esteem you have, the less you have to try harder. If you truly don't think you can do something, I promise you that you will live up to your expectations and fail. You must have confidence in yourself to succeed or you won't.

I have a dream...
- Martin Luther King, Jr.

The difficult we do immediately;
the impossible takes a bit longer.
- US Armed Forces Slogan

Everyone has dreams for a better future.

Your self esteem will determine if they come true or not.

Self Esteem is a belief in yourself. It's respecting the person you are and recognizing that you are responsible for all you are and are not. The world we live in looks for accomplishments and we are judged accordingly. No one can just *be*. Worthiness is determined by what we've done to deserve it, not by who we are. Some things we accomplish and succeed; with other things we make mistakes and fail. Either way, we are neither our successes nor our failures. Who we really are, our intrinsic self, is separate from the mistakes we make along the way. Errors are how we grow. When we learn the lesson the mistake has to offer, we turn each failure into a success. It's up to us to grasp the message in the lesson.

Our interpretation of how life affects us

determines what we think is possible for us.

How we view what happens to us sets our limitations. We give meaning to experiences based on assumptions which we believe to be true, but in fact may not be true at all. The various meanings we assign to these events determine the amount of impact they will have on how we see things. If we determine it to be negative, we feel bad about ourselves and others. If we feel it is positive, it expands our possibilities. When we get beyond our self judgments, opinions, and erroneous evidence, what we have left is what we can become.

One experience of mine was being employed as a shrink wrapper. The company packaged potpourri in just about any type of container. The finishing touch was to encase it in shrink wrap. Since wrap shrinks at its own rate, you can't hasten it. If you leave the heat gun in one place too long, it doesn't shrink faster, it simply burns a hole. My first day on the job I managed to get by without burning too many holes in the plastic wrap. I felt pretty good about myself, after all I was learning a new craft. The second day production increased and time became a factor. I felt I had done pretty good the day before so I could afford to work faster. I ended up burning holes all day. At quitting time, I felt like quitting. I felt the job was beyond my limits, more than I could do well. However I needed

*We do not see things as they are;
we see things as we are.*
- Talmud

To be in hell is to drift,
to be in heaven is to steer.
- George Bernard Shaw

an income so the next day I was back at my station vowing to do better. I worked slower and did just fine. By the time I did quit that job, I could shrink wrap anything, handle any problem. If I had let the second day determine my limits, I would have decided that I was not capable of learning a job that I was later an expert at doing in record time. I would have formed an incorrect opinion based on erroneous evidence.

You determine what your Self is worth.

If you have low self esteem, you don't think you're worth much and often think you are worthless, *worth less*, less than anyone else. You decide what the perfect you would be like, and then you find that you are not able to measure up to that perfection you have arbitrarily set up in the first place.

We think others must also see this terrible lack and judge us to be a far cry from where we are supposed to be. *Yet the measuring stick we're using is one seen only by ourselves.* No one else knows about it. Still we think we have fallen far short of what others must expect. In the end, value judgment just creates more stress for us.

When we believe we can experience more good things in life, we generate experiences in that direction.

Drifting is easy. If you want success, you can't do business as usual. Expect nothing and you will get nothing. Your life will remain the same. Having no direction leads nowhere. Doing just enough to make quota, gives you a lifestyle that just meets your needs and nothing more.

If you have high expectations but see no progress in that direction, it's often because you need to make room in your life by letting go of something. Holding on to opposing thoughts creates limits which obstruct and restrict what you can experience. Once something has served its purpose, it needs to be released to make room for new opportunities. If you want a new wardrobe and your closet is stuffed with clothes you no longer wear, you need to let go of the old to have room for the new. Similarly the same holds true when you want progress and change in your life.

Where there is life, there is hope.
- Terence

The words of the tongue
should have three
gatekeepers.
- Arab proverb

We each have the same hours per day for our use. Some amount of time must be used for sleeping, for eating, for personal activities. The balance is taken up with whatever our preferences are. Most of us have every waking hour already filled with some task. If we want to begin something new in our lives, there won't be room for it until we let go of something already in place.

As the old saying goes, something has to give. Spend less time commuting, relaxing, working, playing, socializing, sleeping. It doesn't matter which area you choose, but choose you must. No matter how you divide it up, you can't make more hours in any day. Just like everyone else, you have 24 hours. To add something new, something old must go to make room in your 24 hour day. Or you will have no time for it to happen.

If you want to travel more but are afraid of flying and dislike driving, you can't hold onto opposites and expect something to happen. Either get over the fear of flying or the long haul of driving, or give up the idea of traveling. If you want to climb the corporate ladder of success but lack the self confidence needed for public speaking, then either get happy with a lower rung that requires less ability or take the steps to gain the confidence you need. Your limitations become obstructions that restrict you. They are self imposed obstacles. You can choose to release them.

When we know and value our own self worth,

no one can make us feel "less than."

Speech has an impact on our lives. Few of us are aware of just how powerful our words are. An encounter with someone can leave us feeling slighted, not respected. The truth is, however, that no one can make us feel bad without our permission. You must agree to be insulted. If someone extends their hands offering you garbage and you don't take it, they're stuck with it. Similarly, they can try to insult you, but if you refuse to take the insult, it doesn't work. You have to agree that the words the other person has uttered have meaning and allow it to have an impact on you. Otherwise, what has been said becomes meaningless and without power. Think about it. If someone insults you in a language or mannerism that is unknown to you, you can't feel insulted because it has no meaning to you. It means nothing. You literally don't get it.

19

The difference between a smart person and a wise person is that a smart person knows what to say and a wise person knows whether or not to say it.
- Quote found on the wall of a recreation center office in Berkeley, CA.

Plan to be spontaneous tomorrow.

Words are powerless until *you* empower them.

Every morning we all need a reason to get out of bed. Our bodies were made for action. Without action they will cease to function. As we get older though, we sometimes begin to feel the stress of all those things that demand our attention. We can't control people or situations outside of ourselves, but we can choose to control our thoughts which are attracting those things we don't want.

You do this by learning to monitor your thoughts. When you find yourself feeling negative, check your thought process. What have you been thinking about? Filter your thoughts, reject any that do not align with the future you desire. One negative thought leads to another unless you take control of what you are thinking. Select only positive thoughts, purposely steering your thinking away from anything negative.

All things begin in the mind with a thought.

Even with just one thought, we start sending out the energy to bring something into existence. Our thoughts tend to wander most of the day, sending little spurts of energy out but not enough to amount to anything. Wandering thoughts don't tend to produce much. Our thoughts need a focal point. Since our thoughts never cease, wouldn't it be better if we directed those thoughts and came up with things we wanted? Our thoughts either revolve around the mundane or rise to new accomplishments. If our experiences are not quite what we had in mind, we may need to realign our thoughts closer to our desires. We impact our environment with our thoughts, feelings, and emotions, just as others affect us. We are never sure of how much we affect one another, but be assured we do with each encounter we have.

The choice you have every day is whether you will choose to be surrounded by a positive atmosphere or envelop yourself in negativity. Every day you must choose. The choice is yours moment by moment. You can even choose to start your day over at any time. You might post a note to yourself on the bathroom mirror stating in no uncertain terms "Today is going to be a good day!" Should something go wrong, it does not dictate that the rest of the day will now be terrible. You have control over that. Decide the negativity ends right then – at that moment – and there – with that situation. Got that?

> *When you see it right and when you feel it right*
> *in the wholeness of your being,*
> *you then have created the condition*
> *that makes the result inevitable.*
> *- Stretton Smith,*
> *The 4T Prosperity Program*

Success is not a destination that we ever reach.
Success is the quality of the journey.
- Jennifer James

A good method of remembering to do this is by carrying a totem in your pocket. It can be anything that pleases you. A simple polished stone does nicely. In *The Secret* they mention taking a plain river stone and calling it a Gratitude Rock. Whenever something happens that you perceive as negative, hold the totem in your hand and think of something positive instead, something you are grateful for in your life. Remember the moment it happened. That indescribable, overwhelming feeling of joy you felt. The more you can feel it, the faster the positive energy you are generating will turn things around. Think of one thing, then another, and another, until you feel your mood change. If you continue to do this, you can end any effects a negative event is having on you. You can choose to remain in a positive mood and environment by being aware and using this practice. It can change your life and others. Even one person with a positive attitude can affect an entire group.

Your thoughts mold your world. Reject the negative, focus on the positive, and you will attract positive people and situations into your life. As long as you are aware of the direction your thoughts are going, you can control them and thus control the attraction to you of constructive and destructive situations in life.

If you wonder what you've been thinking,
take a look around at what is in your life.

If you like what you are getting, keep doing what you are doing. If not, change it. It is only by changing your thinking that you will change your life.

We live with such random thought patterns that we easily fall into the habit of criticizing ourselves rather than affirming our lives. Things happen, emotions change, words fall out of our mouths. Sometimes that's not a good thing.

Your word has power until you say one thing and do another. From that moment on and each subsequent time you do it, your word continues to lose power until your word means nothing because there is no intention behind it. And everyone knows it. Align your words with your intentions. Say what you mean and mean what you say. Believe in yourself. You must believe in yourself first. All else follows.

No one
can defeat us
unless we first defeat
ourselves.
- Dwight D. Eisenhower

In everything give thanks...
- The Lamsa Bible,
I Thessalonians 5:18

How your journey unfolds is entirely up to You.

The choices we make each day will either bring us closer to success, or further away at day's end. Whatever we give our attention to grows and increases. That which we ignore diminishes and fades out of our lives. We create our own roadblocks when we limit our attitude by unknowingly withholding energy and attention. The more enthusiastic we are about anything, the more energy we give it, the more powerful our word about it becomes to manifest it in reality.

The energy we project with our words has
more power than any particular words we use.

Much of the disharmony in life comes from judging people and situations, as well as making comparisons. We can't control others. We can't change situations that have happened. All we can do is to withhold judgment. That does not mean that we are saying everything is acceptable. But, by not allowing something to affect us, we avoid generating more negative energy which would only continue the ripple of negativity. Comparisons between ourselves and others place everyone's self esteem at risk because we can only change ourselves.

Withholding judgment stops the ripple of negativity.

Experiences, both negative and positive, can take on a new meaning if we assume an attitude of gratitude. Difficult times can be seen as opportunities, learning experiences, or even challenges that we are better off having experienced. Once we have gotten through it, we can choose to hang on to the pain, or take the lesson and let the emotion go.

It's human nature to want to be right.
Would you rather be right or be happy?

What is really going on when we disagree with someone? When others don't see things the same way we do, we resist their opinion because we know ours is right. Being right gives us a sense of satisfaction. The trouble is that we can become so hooked on our own opinion that we are unwilling to be open to other options. We can become so

The art of living is a fine mingling of letting go and hanging on.
 - Havelock Ellis

Even when a situation seems so personal, even if others insult you directly, it has nothing to do with you.

- Don Miguel Ruiz

self-centered that our egos insist on being right. We want things done the right way, which is of course our way.

Lou was visiting his mother. Taking a walking tour of the front yard, she pointed out to him a problem she was having. The drip tube for the water condensation from the air conditioning unit was producing a puddle of water near the foundation of the house. Analyzing the situation, Lou realized that there was enough of the drip tube exposed to allow a connection for a drip irrigation system. That would not only remove the puddle, it would accomplish watering the front yard garden at the same time. He told her he would fix it, bought the parts, and installed a 50 ft. drip irrigation system to water every plant in the garden. It took two hours but he felt it was worth it. He was proud of what he had accomplished and showed his mother. She looked, he explained, and she complained. It was too much. The water would never reach all the plants. In brief, she hated it.

Lou couldn't believe it. After he had spent all this time and trouble to put in a whole system, she didn't want it! At first he was angry. He had tried to do something nice and it wasn't even appreciated. Well, if she didn't want it, he would tear it out. But as he began removing the drip lines, he realized that he wasn't doing her a favor by giving her more than she wanted. It was a favor if he did what *she* wanted, not what *he* wanted. So instead of removing all of it, he simplified it to a single short drip line that she could easily move from plant to plant watering each individually. When he showed her the scaled down version, she was happy, pleased, and thanked him for all of his efforts.

The question is: just how much is being right worth?

Lou's mom had a habit of saying, "I always get what I want." She was very proud of that. It doesn't sound bad until you realize that the necessary corollary means no one else gets what they want, ever, unless it happens to be in agreement with her wishes.

Getting your way feels good, but if what you are doing is not what the other person had in mind, what's the point? Just how important and fragile is your own ego? If you want to be appreciated for your efforts, then you must be willing to do what the other person wants. That makes them happy. Or you can insist on being right....happy now?

You were not made for failure, no matter who you are,
nor how much you know, nor what anyone has told you.
- Emma Curtis Hopkins

---

*We can easily forgive a child who is afraid of the dark;
the real tragedy of life is when men are afraid of the
light. - Plato*

You can often feel like your self confidence is at risk if suddenly you find you're wrong. You then lose confidence in yourself to be right. The more others disagree with you, the worse you feel. You may look for confirmation from someone else when you have an important decision to make.

Years ago there used to be truth in advertising. When something was being sold, a claim could not be made unless it was true. You could trust what was being said. Well, "used to" is the operative phrase here. Something happened to that law. It seems to have gone away when no one was looking. Advertising now seems to include saying anything that will sell the item. If you've been anywhere near internet marketing, you'll hear a thousand and one offers on how to do it and make tons of money. Do you believe them or not?

Someone says it will work. You believe him. It doesn't. You get scammed. Then you try another, still trying to believe, to trust the person is telling you the truth. But you wonder if you're right. You think you are, but also thought you were last time, and you were wrong. So you ask a couple of friends for second opinions. They wonder if you're still sane. That starts you wondering too if you have lost your mind. You start doubting yourself, second guessing yourself. Your self confidence is bound to take a dive. You're headed for a world of trouble if you start feeling like you can't trust yourself again to be right, to make a good decision.

To solve the problem, you must regain confidence in yourself. Self confidence is the key, the beginning, the cornerstone for success to be built on. Now is when you need to enforce it. An easy way to increase your self confidence is by listening to subliminal messages. Scientifically done, they change your mind to think positive thoughts about yourself. A company I would recommend is Alphasonics International. I know their products work, all you have to do is listen.

The first step is believing in yourself, all the way. With all your faults and mistakes, and your talents and abilities. Know you can do it, and you will be able to do it. Believe in yourself. Have confidence in yourself, in your strength. Self confidence that is strong will keep you together and help you shine. All else follows from there.

When spring comes,
the grass grows by
itself.
- Zen Master
Yun-men

To the world
you may be one person,
but to one person
you may be the world.
- Rabbi Joseph Heller

Life is in us all the time;
we think all the time;
we are continually
creating our tomorrows.
- Ernest Holmes,
A New Design for Living

Chapter 3

In the Beginning

*I*n the beginning when we first encounter this world as babies, we find our predominate needs met. At the earliest, our needs are very basic: survival and comfort. In order to survive, we need food and shelter; for comfort, clothing. In addition to this, most of us get a few bonuses in the form of love and attention. Most of us find ourselves in the lap of approval.

When we cry out to make our needs known,

we not only get food, get dry, get comfortable,

we also get hugs and kisses and smiles.

All to make us feel good.

If we don't feel good, someone generally comes along, fixes that, and once more we're happy and pretty content with life as we know it. Our awareness consists mainly of our instincts. As we grow, heredity begins to have an effect on us in our appearance. How we appear to others in turn affects how we are treated which brings into play our life experiences.

We have no value system until we are exposed to one.

Everything has beauty,
but not everyone sees it.
- Confucius

If you do not stand for
something, you will fall for
anything.

Early on everything is pretty much the same to us. To a child, playing with a string is the same as playing with a costly necklace of gold. One has no more value than the other; they have the same worth and for a child they are the same, except one is shiny. As we grow we learn to place a value on things, item by item, as we are exposed to the opinions and value systems of our peers and others.

Often we have determined

the significance or importance of something,

without realizing that its worth is based on the opinion of someone else.

How many times have you seen children hold onto something, considering it of great value, until an adult or peer comes along and calls it junk. In most instances, this information is accepted as fact, the item reclassified, and then discarded as worthless. Children learn values based on the opinion of another, because someone they respected said so. The child has been told to respect that person, so their opinion and values must be right.

The value may be sound or not.

You can see how easily everyone can acquire a distorted view of anything. If you believe someone, you accept their belief system as correct. As a child, anyone older than you becomes an authority figure who you assume must be right. Without knowing it or intending it, you then may make an incorrect assumption based on a belief system that may be extremely uninformed or biased. That's how prejudices get passed down through generations of family and friends. You hear it so it must be right, and you go along with it. Anyone can have an opinion about anything; that doesn't make it right though.

As we get older, we learn to make our own observations. If they are free of value judgments and free of emotional attachment, what we perceive will be closer to a factual representation of reality.

Learning brings a confusion of praise,

reward, blame, and punishment.

When you stop comparing
what is right here and now
with what you wish were,
you can begin to enjoy
what is.
- Cheri Huber

Sometimes we seek too much information
and not enough transformation. - Sai Baba

We first encounter appreciation when we are infants. Others respond favorably to us simply because they acknowledge us as new beings here to learn and grow. We continue to be appreciated, admired, approved of, liked and loved, because someone recognizes in us something that pleases them. We aren't old enough yet where our actions are liable to merit much praise or punishment. We can smile at someone and be loved just for that.

As the years go by, however, we are taught various actions and expected to perform them. Appreciation for just existing starts to exit from our lives. The world begins to expect more of us. Now we can be rewarded or punished because of factual observations of our characteristics, actions, and learning ability. Praise and blame become factors. When we do something well, we like to hear praise for what we've done. When something wrong happens, the blame game may begin. We can get caught up in finding a scapegoat for the incident, trying to place the blame elsewhere to exonerate ourselves from any culpability, rather than be intent on finding the solution.

Some of us can never get past the blame. These are the people we know who state the problem and then rehash it over and over. They get stuck on finding someone to blame for the problem and never get around to finding the solution. It's easier to stay in the negative rather than work in the positive. Finding a solution requires more effort. Then repetitive recitations turns blaming into complaining. The rehash goes on and on as long as there is someone willing to listen to the negative chatter.

When we have done an excellent job, we feel good about ourselves. We would be much better off if we could just leave it at that, and sometimes we can. However, often we do things we don't especially want to do because we are in the market for praise and appreciation. It's nice to be acknowledged, to hear a "thank you" for our efforts when we do something for someone. Should we fail to receive it, the good we felt from doing the job seems to slip away from us. Instead of feeling good, we can feel bitter. Looking for approval, acting as a people pleaser, can lead to resentment. While appreciation is thoughtful acknowledgment and gratitude for a job well done, praise becomes a manipulative factor embracing the ego. Only the person being praised feels good. Anyone else involved may feel "less than" the person receiving the praise. On the other hand, appreciation lifts everyone's self esteem. Bottom line, when you do something for someone, do it because you want to, not because you are looking for approval.

Your vision will become clear only
when you look into your heart.
Who looks outside, dreams.
Who looks inside awakens.
- Carl Jung

Security is mostly a superstition. It does not exist in nature,
nor do the children of men as a whole experience it. Avoiding
danger is no safer in the long run than outright exposure.
Life is either a daring adventure or nothing.
- Helen Keller

Ida and Bess traveled out of state to visit their mother. Bess spent hours outside doing gardening which was difficult for her mother to do, but was also using this tactic to avoid long discussions. Ida got along better with their mother so stayed inside talking with her. Mom constantly praised Bess' actions to Ida while protesting that she didn't want Bess working. Ida became torn between obeying her mother's wishes and not doing things that she said she didn't want to have done, or being like Bess and doing them anyway. She tried a compromise by continually asking if she could help with anything. Her offer was always refused. In the end, Bess was praised for doing things and actually going against her mom's stated wishes and Ida was made to feel that she wasn't doing enough even though she did what her mother asked. When Ida did do something, it was wrong or not as good as Bess could do. If gratitude had simply been expressed, then both girls would have felt good. Instead, praise and comparison were used. By the end of the visit, Bess felt terrific and Ida felt terrible. She felt less worthy due to a loss of self esteem.

Every time we make a mistake,
we identify with our actions and blame ourselves.

We learn this as children when the voice of authority states that we have done something wrong and puts us down for what we have done. We hear it. We accept it. This is usually the beginning of our lack of self esteem. Parents often continue this practice even after their children have become adults. Sometimes knowingly, sometimes unknowingly.

Praise places a judgment value on our performance identifying us with our actions. If we do less than perfect, we automatically are set up for blame. We are made to feel bad about our actions. Guilt erodes our self esteem. If others don't blame us, we soon learn to put ourselves down for our own mistakes, defeats, failures, and bad decisions. We forget that we are not our actions. Unless our perception of reality changed our perspective of the situation, the outcome could not have been different. We can only be as wise as we are aware. If nothing changes, nothing changes.

Low self esteem makes us vulnerable
to the opinions and attitudes of others.

Refuse

to put yourself down.

Choose

to believe yourself capable.

> We differ from
> others only in what
> we do and don't do -
> not in what we are.
> - Anthony DeMello

Low self esteem makes you feel like you have no self worth unless someone praises you. This makes receiving praise a necessity. Your sense of worth becomes dependent on the opinion of others. Without it you feel *less than,* inferior, worth less than everyone else. When you put yourself down or allow someone else to, you can't feel good about yourself. Many of us operate from a conditioned need for approval and acceptance which generates anxiety. We are under pressure to constantly do as well as we have been doing, or better, to continually deserve the praise we are seeking. This can make us defensive of our actions and resentful of the pressure. Praise sometimes implies surprise that we were able to do as well as we did. It also can foster resentment if we expect praise and receive no recognition for our efforts. Doing things for the sake of praise can result in anxiety, as it implies a need to be validated by others. Self esteem is threatened when our authority and sense of worth are compromised. With sound self esteem, we know our value is innate , not something to be earned.

No one needs anyone else's opinion to validate his worth.

Each of us has a perception of reality that is different from anyone else's. Your awareness formed from your heredity, instinct, and experiences will be all your own. Comparison to others is therefore an invalid exercise, even though we often do it.

Praise is tricky. It is important because it makes us feel good, makes us try harder. Even when you know you've done your best, just the thought of trying harder changes the input, which will change the result. What *is* your best becomes what *was* your best as you assume the fact is correct – that you are capable of doing even better than your best. Another level of success is produced because you believed that it could be so. It's important to give praise, it helps us to do better. We need to hear praise without comparison to anyone else, to hear it just because a good job was done.

We could learn a lot from crayons:
some are sharp, some are pretty,
some are dull, some have weird names,
and all are different colors
but they all have to learn to live
in the same box.

Man is what he believes.
- Anton Chekov

Better keep yourself clean and
bright;
you are the window
through which you must see
the world.
- George Bernard Shaw

Chapter 4

The Fall of Self Esteem

Why Do You Lose It?

When we indulge in the human tendency that we are all guilty of doing at some time, to criticize ourselves and what we do, we make ourselves feel less worthy. Each time we engage in criticizing ourselves, we endanger our self esteem and with it goes caring about ourselves, taking care of ourselves, loving ourselves.

When we criticize ourselves and determine

that we haven't measured up to our own standards,

we find ourselves worth less than we felt we were worth before.

You can see a person's level of self esteem reflected in how well he takes care of himself. Have you ever seen an addict who looked like he had good self esteem? If your self esteem is in good shape, you think enough of yourself, love your Self enough, to take care of your body. An unkempt person is a sign of self esteem at less than zero. This must change before anything else is possible. The more self esteem you have the better you feel about yourself, and most likely, the better you will take care of your body. Not taking care of yourself is contradictory to having good self esteem. One necessarily follows the

In the sky, there is no distinction of east and west.
People create the distinctions out of their own minds,
and then believe them to be true.
- The Teachings of Buddha

Only you can deprive yourself of anything.
Do not oppose this realization,
for it is truly the beginning
of the dawn of light.
- A Course in Miracles

other. The ultimate act of low self esteem is suicide – the termination of a self that one can no longer tolerate.

The more we refuse to accept a negative experience,
the more self-destructive emotion we generate.

If we choose to perceive something as negative, that choice has the power to hurt us. Although it doesn't feel like it, we control how much something can hurt us. We can make it as big and encompassing, or small and inconsequential as we want. If you lose your favorite ring or pen, how much power do you give the event? Do you let it ruin your entire day, or do you let your annoyance go as quickly as you can? Anytime we allow something to hurt us, our self esteem is at risk. Total unconditional acceptance of one's self is a basic requirement of sound self esteem.

We judge anything, and everything.
How do we stop judging? It's all about choice.

There's an effect, a reaction, for every action you take. The consequence of the action, negative or positive, is what happens to you. Whether you perceive it as good or bad, is all relative. What is good for someone else, may not be so good for you. What is good in one case, may not be good in another. Know that whatever your reaction in any situation, it was the best you could do, otherwise you would have done something else. Your decision can change with different input. You will always make the only and best choice possible with whatever current information you have available.

One Sunday afternoon I went into in a fast food restaurant to pick up my order. The place was busy – a dozen cars in the drive-thru and customers inside backed up three deep. The staff of four teenagers were doing their best, hurrying as fast as possible. One of the girls came to the counter, put an order down on it and shouted a number. No one came forward. She said it again. Still no one came. Her face filled with exasperation and annoyance as she shouted the number even louder one more time. Another girl came over to her and quietly said, "That number is at the window. It's a drive-up." Her look changed to one of consternation and then understanding. She walked over to the window

43

No one ever built a monument to a critic.
- George Bernard Shaw

The innermost essence of our being is beyond ego.
It is fearless; it is free; it is immune to criticism;
it does not fear any challenge.
- Deepak Chopra,
The Seven Spiritual Laws of Success

with a smile. She had been doing her best to reach that customer, shouting the number several times, but she was not achieving the correct result. When the information changed, she was able to change her actions. Then because her best changed, she succeeded. All because the input changed, her action changed and so the result changed.

We pass judgment
when people don't measure up to the way
we think they should perform.

In addition to ourselves and our own actions upsetting us, an additional source of conflict is created when we engage in criticizing others. Even though our backgrounds and experiences are totally different, we still think others should behave the same way we would. We think that behavior would be correct action. We judge others, compare them to the way we think they should be, and sometimes find them lacking. Any action we don't like, we see as a threat to how we feel about ourselves. It contains the possibility that for some reason we're wrong when we thought we were right.

If I don't like what you are doing, that means you are doing something I don't think you should be doing. Yet, since you are doing it, obviously you think you should. One of us *has* to be wrong if we aren't agreeing on the correctness of your actions. The point is, why does our sense of worth feel threatened when someone doesn't agree with us? We even have the tendency to search for someone else who does agree with us. Why do most of us need that support? Why does it matter? And again, do we want to be right or be happy?

If we are unable to recognize and accept our own authority
to think and do as we choose,
we continue to need the confirmation from others that we are right.

When others agree with us, we feel justified. Anyone who disagrees with us threatens our self worth because we're suddenly in the wrong. We think something must be the matter with us and that threatens our self esteem. The more confirmation is sought from

45

A smile is the universal language of
the acceptance of one another
unconditionally.
- Lenny Ravich

Laugh often,
long and loud.
Laugh until you
gasp for breath.

others, the less we recognize our own authority, ability, and self worth. With low self esteem when someone doesn't agree with us, we simply judge them wrong; that makes us right again, erroneously establishing that we are always right and seldom wrong.

Passing judgment generally makes you feel good for the moment, but judging something to be negative is the only way that something can have a negative effect on you. Your totally optional judgment call gives it power over you and how you feel. Everything is neutral until you decide to pass judgment. Once it's been judged negative, it can be detrimental to you. Truth is, it has no power of its own. It just *is*.

I was expecting an email from an old friend. I wasn't sure I was going to like the reply – rough translation: I wasn't sure I was going to hear what I wanted to hear. I had only moments to glance at the response. Scanning it, I didn't see the words I was looking for. I closed the email, feeling upset. While I had no clear idea of what it actually said, I had decided all on my own that it was a negative response and let it upset me. I refused to read it again for weeks. I didn't want to confirm what I wanted to deny. When I thought I had finally reached a neutral feeling about it, I opened it again. On careful reading I discovered that while it wasn't exactly what I had wanted to hear, it also wasn't negative at all. By needlessly passing judgment I had succeeded in upsetting myself for weeks for no good reason. If I had simply chosen to not label it bad, it would have had no affect on me. It had been my choice to hurt myself.

You give it power by changing its neutral position

to positive or negative according to how much you feel

it can benefit you or hurt you.

The act of thinking of something as negative is a threat to feeling good and in fact is the only way to start feeling bad. Only by thinking of something as negative does it become negative. It is neutral until we label it good or bad. It's all in how we think of it.

You can't change what's happening,

but you *can* stop thinking of something as bad.

One love. One heart.
Let's get together and feel all right.
- Bob Marley

*Out beyond ideas of wrong doing and right doing
there is a field.
I 'll meet you there some day.
- Rumi*

Everyone loses a job sometime. Some see it as negative, the end of their world. Others see it as positive, an opportunity for a new experience. If we would simply stop labeling something as bad, it would remain neutral having no affect on us, or possibly even be seen as positive. When we feel good about ourselves, our self esteem is secure.

We always think that our perception of reality is right.

Anyone who doesn't think like we do, *should* because we're right. Yet our perception of reality is determined by our heredity, instincts, and experiences. No two people can have the same exact perception of reality. There are too many variables for it to be possible.

All emotion, no matter how intensely projected outward, by necessity has to be felt by the one projecting it.

If you love someone, you feel that love before you show it. If you hate someone, you also must experience that hate, feel it, before you can project it at that person. Try this exercise: Think of someone in your life who you don't like. If you hate this person for doing or not doing something to you, recall everything you can about the reason, the moment, the action. Dredge up every horrible detail. Now check how your feelings have changed. If you have done a really good job on bringing this person to life and the reason you feel the way you do, you are now experiencing negative feelings.

Now think of someone that you love. Recall everything about this person – looks, personality, favorite memories. The more you can remember, the more you will begin to feel the emotion of love that you connect with this person. You experience the love before you project that feeling to that person or anyone else. Recall any intense experience with any person and you will see that you must feel the emotion before you can express it or project it. Feelings of love or hate must be experienced by yourself first and, in doing so, you either benefit or suffer even before you can project any of those feelings.

When we love someone, everything they do we see as good. Should that person do something we think is bad, we then tend to judge them as bad right along with their action. While it seems that the negativity falls on them, in actuality it falls on us as we are

There are no mistakes;
just creative ways of
doing things.

In the realm of Nature
there is nothing
purposeless, trivial, or unnecessary.
- Maimonides

denying ourselves the opportunity to feel good. Once we judge someone we love as bad, we can't help but feel bad too. Yet the person, who has become the target of our emotions, always has the option of whether or not to accept what we are projecting. On the other hand, when *we* are on the receiving end, we often forget that option and just accept whatever is being thrown at us as if we didn't have the choice of whether or not to accept it or feel it.

We need to practice living in unconditional love rather than judgment, allowing a person to be who and what they are and just *be*. Agreeing to living in unconditional love does not mean an unconditional relationship or unconditional trust. It means a loving acceptance and respect for each person as he is at that present moment. None of us are perfect. We must trust that each person is learning and growing according to their own perfect timetable. Each experience is exactly how it should be, when it should be. With no judgment, there is no hate, and so nothing to forgive.

Things happening in our lives that upset us, we think of as *unwanted* events or situations.

By doing so, we label them as negative. We want it to be otherwise, yet it can't be other than what it is. Actually, it is neutral until we make it personal. We decide by a value judgment if it is to be considered good or bad. We can't stop an event from happening. We *can* determine it's influence on us. We can leave it neutral, without effect, or change it to good or bad by our own independent decision.

Marcie decided to buy an air conditioner. When she got to the store she found they were sold out even though just a few days before they had over a dozen of them. She was so upset she asked to speak to the store manager who found out that they had some in another store. That was the good news. The bad news was that they were not able to do a store transfer for her, and worse, the store was over an hour away in another city. When she told her husband the news, he was furious and told her to complain. She knew that complaining would do no good. It was what it was and no amount of yelling at someone would change a thing except to upset her even more. Her options were limited. She didn't want to drive the hour but she needed the item. She realized she could choose to remain upset, drive for an hour while stewing over the situation which would only make

To everything there is a season,
and time for every purpose under the sun;
a time to be born, a time to die;
a time to plant and a time to reap...
- Ecclesiastes 3:1-2

The journey of thousand miles begins with
a broken fan belt and a leaking tire.

it worse and her more miserable, or she could simply decide to make the drive, put on some music, enjoy the scenery, and put the aggravation out of her mind. Either way the drive had to be made. It was her choice whether or not to give the situation the power to upset her.

The incident was neutral. She gave it the power to upset her at first, and then chose to change her thinking to remove that power. With her attitude change she then continued on the positive path by choosing to enjoy the ride as much as she could, rather than fume at the rush hour traffic and the hours she had to spend driving. She realized it was to her benefit both to go ahead with the purchase and dismiss the inconvenience. She would only be hurting herself to do otherwise.

If you let it remain neutral, it has no effect on you.

Don't make it personal, when it isn't.

If you judge something that has happened to you as unfair, it is no longer neutral. Instantly, you have given it the power to change how you feel. It becomes a negative event in your mind and any good feelings you had are now gone. When that happens remember then that you can change your attitude at any time.

For example, you're driving your car on a highway. You check your rearview mirror and see a car approaching. A few minutes later, the car is tailgating you. Just when you start to get annoyed, the car changes lanes. Than a few seconds later, it cuts in front of you. Instead of keeping the same speed and getting out of your way, the driver slows down. "Why?" you ask. You wonder why he's out to get you. What's his problem? If you are self-obsessed, then your thoughts turn towards yourself, "that it must be all about me!"

The fact is that he most likely isn't even aware of you, or how his driving is affecting you. The event is totally neutral, unless you make it and take it personally. Making it personal is how road rage starts.

At some point in each of our lives, we all experience the end of something that means a great deal to us. It could be the death of a relationship, a person, or perhaps a pet. Part of the human experience is to become attached to people and animals in our lives.

Somehow, in the midst of our tears, a gift is hidden.
Somehow, in the midst of our mourning, the first
steps of the dance take place. - Henri Nouwen

Take up the song;
forget the epitaph.
- Edna St Vincent Millay

Day after day they are a part of our lives, then one day they aren't. They're gone and there is nothing that we can do to bring them back. How does one cope?

If you let adversity win, you let it have power over you. All you will see is another bad thing happening. You will feel terrible, then you'll start to deny, refuse to accept it, fight against having it happen. But it can't not happen. An event that has taken place, can't be undone. The only thing you can do is accept it. Let it go. Find a way to rise above it. Find the good in it. Like a many-faceted crystal, if you keep turning it and looking at it from another viewpoint, eventually you'll be able to find a small bit of good. It may be infinitesimal. It may be only that the time you spent together was well spent. It may be only that you now have some good memories. Do this and you will find there's good in every situation.

Take a positive attitude no matter what.
You know what will happen?

Your self esteem will rise, expand, and you will feel so good that nothing will bother you. That's what high Self Esteem is... the ability to feel really good about yourself no matter what is going on in your life.

If you agree to allow something to be without judgment, you still haven't changed what has taken place, but you have removed the possibility of it hurting you. That's taking your power back, supporting yourself, and it will increase your self esteem. If you can't stop reality from happening – and you can't – all you can do is to *let it be*. Accept that it has happened and let it go.

No experience lasts forever
unless you hang onto that negative experience.

You can allow the experience to remain, to take root and continue to grow within you. You can give it space to live in your mind. Give it a corner to smolder in, or nurture it until it becomes your every thought, your very life. You are giving the experience "free rent" in your head.

One should count
each day
a separate life.
- Seneca

It's important to see the relationship
between thoughts of fear and lack and how
they manifest themselves as experiences
appearing as if someone or something is
against you.
- Gary Simmons, *The I of the Storm*

We all start off equal as children. As adults, some of us are positive folks seeing the best in things as much as we can. Others have become wearisome entities – negative, complaining, bitching and moaning about how bad things are. Few of us have a constant barrage of experiences that are totally negative or positive, yet something causes us to change into one kind of person or the other. We can end up thinking we must not be good enough.

You allow it to happen.

Letting something continue to be a constant negative

is an agreement to hurt yourself.

When our life experiences seem to be one bad thing after another, we have a tendency to become a negative thinking person. It's hard to be anything else. Usually at some point though, things change. But we can be so wrapped up in our negativity that we fail to notice it. As far as we are concerned, everything is still bad everywhere we look. We hang on to that negativity because that's the way we're used to thinking. We think ourselves into a negative rut without realizing that we are the cause of that rut. And all that rut does is hurt us. It keeps us from seeing and experiencing anything positive. This can happen from one end of the spectrum to the other, for any one of us.

You can lose your job, lose your partner, lose your home, wreck your car. Now you have no income, no place to live, no means of transportation, and no one who cares any of this is happening to you. Opportunities to change any of these circumstances can be thrown at your feet but you will fail to see them, if all you can see now are bad things happening to you. You will miss any good that is trying to take place in your life and continue to attract negative things to you instead. If you are negative, then you attract negative things. When you change into a more positive thinking person, both the people around you change along with the type of opportunities you attract.

Sometimes negative experiences are a call for change in the world. If we see something that we feel we have no choice but to judge it and know it to be bad, then we need to do something about it. Some actions are evil no matter how you look at them. Adults that prey on children, mistreat animals, find pleasure in hurting other living beings

Accept your feelings as
natural;
learn from them;
let them pass through you;
get on with your life.
- Dan Millman,
Everyday Enlightenment

See the past as it was,
but don't re-emotionalize it.
- Raymond Charles Barker, *Barkerisms*

in our world create circumstances that shout for change. These things should not be ignored. They should be addressed so that they will end. The important thing is to take action but not take it personally. If you make it personal all it does is bring your feelings into play. Once your emotions become involved, you're opening yourself to being hurt. Create change in the world, make it a better place, but do it without endangering yourself. Act with passion, but leave your emotions out of it because that only succeeds in dragging you into a position of being hurt.

Men and women coming home from fighting a war are filled with negative memories. They have seen things that they wish they could erase from their minds. Mental pictures that anyone who wants to maintain their sanity wants to be rid of forever. Some succeed in crossing back over the line and grabbing hold of one good experience after another until they can build a bridge back to a positive framework. Others remain stuck in the past unable to let go of the ruin they have seen. They carry that past negativity with them and let it become their present as well. They think, "this is who I am, so therefore I must act based upon how I feel."

No matter how you feel about it, you can't change what is happening. Not calling something bad doesn't make it good, but it can remove the emotional charge. Your natural state is to be positive, content with the world around you. When you see something as negative, it will put you out of balance. As a result you become unhappy, and unwittingly place your self esteem at risk. You can't change reality. You do have the power to change your attitude.

Change how you look at things, how you feel about things, your reaction to the actions of others, and you will change your attitude. With a change of attitude, your life will also automatically change. Change your actions. Act "as if" it already is so. You don't think your way into right acting; you act your way into right thinking.

> *To men*
> *some things are good and some are bad.*
> *But to God,*
> *all things are good and beautiful and just.*
> *- Heraclitus*

If the present
tries to sit in judgment
of the past,
it will lose the future.
- Winston Churchill

A child of five could understand this.
Fetch me a child of five.
- Groucho Marx

Chapter 5

It's All Relative

$\mathcal{T}$he world we see around us simply *is*. Neither good nor bad until we place a value judgment on it. Once we interpret a neutral event to be negative, we give it power over us. Now it can make us feel bad in some way. Although we are powerless to alter an event that has already taken place, we can learn from it and avoid having it happen in the future.

If we criticize, blame or find fault with something,

we have formed a negative value judgment.

A negative value judgment results in the decision, "it was bad." That opens two options to us: we can accept it and let it go, or choose to not accept it and allow it to keep upsetting us. If we refuse to accept it, or are unwilling to pay the price to change it, all we accomplish is to make ourselves feel bad, generate more negative energy, and lose any good feelings we might have had. A neutral or good mood changes into a bad mood, but it doesn't change the reality or make it go away. All it does is give an unwanted event power over how we will feel. Sometimes we encounter a situation that no matter how hard we don't want to judge, it's impossible not to think of it as bad. And sometimes something has to be done about it. It simply can't be dismissed. Then the most important thing to remember is to remove the bond our emotions create and do our best

We are what our thoughts have made us;
so take care about what you think.
- Swami Vivekananda

When we change the way we look at things,
the things we look at change.
- Wayne Dwyer

to solve the problem. Either way the reality doesn't change, because it can't change. But without the emotional tie that binds us, the situation can no longer hurt us. It is the simple act of judgment that gives it the power to make us feel a certain way. The more clearly we see and grasp the meaning of our life's experiences, the more aware we are of what is really going on, the less we find it necessary to judge. The fastest way out of pain and suffering is to not argue with what is, but to look for what is positive about the situation. We came into this physical form to delight in life and learn from it, not suffer through it.

It is *we* who judge something
to be a positive or negative happening in our lives.

Consider rain for a moment. If you are planning a picnic, a rainy day is bad – an unwanted reality you are powerless to change. For another person tending a garden, rain is good. Either way, same rain. Only the attitude is different, and it's all relative. Rain as a reality simply *is*. Fundamentally, it is neither good nor bad. The more we resist that reality that we have decided is negative, the more miserable we make ourselves. Letting it be is a wiser choice. Then there is no resistance. Resistance to a condition tends to make that condition persist because it is getting your attention. We can't change the weather; all we can change is our attitude towards it.

That which has your attention will flourish.
What you ignore dies from lack of interest.

Shower your attention on anything – a plant, an animal, a child, an idea, a friend, a lover. The plant will grow, the animal and child will trust you, your idea will materialize, a relationship will prosper. Yet withdraw your attention and energy from any of these and what was prosperous will wither and die instead. Don't water the plant, or pet the animal, or hug the child, or act on the idea, or call the friend, or see the lover. The result will be the same. All of these can and will be lost due to lack of interest and attention.

Be aware, awake to what is going on in your life. Once you acknowledge it, you can no longer deny it. When you are aware that some choice you have made is not working for you, has had a negative impact on your life, you gain the option of changing it. If you

The "what should be" never did exist,
but people keep trying to live up to it.
There's no "what should be,"
there is only what is.
- Lenny Bruce

Experience is
something you don't
get until just after
you need it.

choose to continue doing it, at least you are aware of what you are doing and you can take responsibility for your actions and whatever continuing reality they create. Or, once aware of what reality you have created, you can opt to change it for a better, positive reality, one that makes you happy. But you can do nothing without being aware of what is going on and how it is affecting you.

Three things in our lives are instrumental in forming our awareness: heredity, instinct, and experience. Our heredity is composed of all the factors we inherit from our biological family. Our natural instinct is that Inner Knowing that we inherently rely on. Our life experience is what happens to us along the way. The first two factors cannot be changed. We enter this world with them and they are what we have to work with during our life. Experience is the only factor we can change in the equation.

Things you don't want in your life, fall into three categories of causes.

You live in a physical world of cause and effect. When something happens to you, it is caused by either yourself, by other people, or by outside events. Each causal event has its own effects.

We all generate our own shoulda, coulda, woulda, didn't moments that we regret, wish we wouldn't have done. Friends, family, and strangers act in ways we don't approve and often cause us misery. We see certain situations as negative events that we would prefer not to have in our lives. Usually, we do not have the power to change these things or if we do, we don't because we are unwilling to pay the price.

Sometimes we really want something to be different, but feel the price is too high to pay for the change. What can we do about it if we can't change it? We can remove the emotional bond by removing the negative spin we have arbitrarily placed on it. Once the emotional tag is gone, the charge fades until it can no longer produce bad feelings.

We can go from feeling bad to feeling okay again, just by changing our perception of it, suspending our judgment.

It takes more than
a sudden leap
to change a life.
It takes a conscious act,
a decision to take our life into
our own hands and really
understand ourselves.
- Mildred Newman

Self-criticism or self-judgment is self-hatred.
It will always hurt you.
There is no exception to that.
- Dick Olney, *Walking in Beauty*

One morning on my way to work, traffic came to a halt due to an accident. Expecting it to be cleared quickly, I waited, preparing myself to remain neutral. As minutes passed and we barely moved, I began to fret, get negative, and become angry. I was going to be late when I purposely started out early. As I felt the emotional charge build, I made the decision to step back for a moment from the situation to get a different perspective. There was absolutely nothing I could do about the problem. There was no other road to take. All I could do was wait. It was totally within my power to be positive or negative. I took a deep breath and looked around. The sun was shining. It was a beautiful day. Why not enjoy it? I had a new CD I hadn't heard yet. I put my window down, turned up the speaker volume, leaned back to bask in the sun, closed my eyes, and took myself away to a better place. A situation that could have been bad was turned around to be positive instead. I was able to actually enjoy a forty-five minute delay during which I traveled only one mile.

It is our decision to make a neutral event negative. Returning it to neutral removes the emotional charge. The event still exists but no longer has the power to cause bad feelings. Unless we make it personal, creating an emotional bond with it, it cannot upset us. We can care about something without emotional attachment, just by changing our perception of it, suspending judgment.

The most common source of low self esteem is

criticizing or condemning ourselves

for not living up to *our own* standards and expectations.

We put ourselves down for our own actions. We operate on needs. What matters to us most will get our attention first. We will always choose to respond to our dominant need. That is how we make all the choices in our lives.

When there is one thing you know you should do, but you perceive another need is greater than that, the greater need is the one on which you will choose to act. You make that choice based on the facts as you know them. Should the information change, i.e., you learn of other contributing factors, your greater need can change. Then you have the option of making a different choice.

Success is getting what you want.
Happiness is wanting what you get.
- Dave Gardner

Liberty means responsibility.
That is why most men dread it.
- George Bernard Shaw, *Liberty*

**Choice changing is always based on new evidence
and re-evaluation of the available facts.**

Suppose you need to be some place at a certain time. You decide on the shortest, fastest route. All is well until you see a flood of brake lights in front of you signaling a massive traffic jam. This is not good. You can now stay and hope the traffic clears quickly or take an alternate route. You can't chance being late, so you choose the other route. Of course you have no way of knowing if this is the better choice or not, and you won't know until you get there and it's too late. It all depends on how much information you have to analyze to make the choice that will give you the best results. If your cell phone rings and a friend informs you that the current road is torn up with construction and it is the worst choice you could make, then the information would enable another choice again.

**For every thing you do,
you make a choice to do it or not to do it.**

If you don't do it, you choose another available option, and that is what you do. You can only do whatever it is that you prefer to do based on your preference at any given time. You'd rather do this than that, and your choice is made. Most importantly, it is your ONLY choice because of how you perceive the situation at that moment. Change the information to your awareness, and you may choose differently.

**No matter how you think or what you do,
you are not your awareness or your actions.**

Our level of awareness is determined by how perceptive our minds are. Our personal perception of the world is received through our senses and analyzed by our minds. The problem is that we tend to erroneously identify with the way we think. This leads us to identify ourselves with our actions. We apply the same illogic to those around us. Thinking bad thoughts doesn't make a person bad. Acting on those thoughts, doesn't make a person bad either. Bad thoughts and actions are simply bad in themselves. They do not make the person bad. It's just a good person doing something he shouldn't.

69

I am not what I want to be, I am
not all that I could be, but thank
God I'm not what I used to be.
- Jack Boland

Life is what happens on the way.
- Southwest Airlines poster

Even though it's our bodies that perform our actions, we are not our actions any more than we are our thoughts. The Inner Spirit, the essence of each person, is separate from all actions and thoughts. We are responsible for them, but they are not us.

Should you do something undesirable or bad, that does not make you a bad person.

Even though the action was bad, it was your faulty perception of the situation that led you to do it, thinking it would result in a positive outcome for you.

Say a man robs a store to get money for medicine that he can't afford but must have to save someone's life. Saving a life is a good thing. Robbing a store is a bad thing. Yet he can't see how to accomplish one and avoid the other. Does that make the man good or bad then? The answer is neither.

The man is not his actions. Only the action is bad. We can argue about the actions, and motivations, and the awareness that caused the actions, but the man himself cannot be called bad for doing what he did.

Your special slant of awareness, how you see the world, is a function your mind performs. It is not you. You are also not what you do. Your actions simply respond to your dominating need which is chosen by your present awareness. If your choices turn out to be bad choices, it doesn't make you bad. It just means the choice was bad and consequently the action was bad. How you see the world around you affects how you think.

If your thinking is faulty, it is because your perception of reality is faulty.

Each of us is a perfect being inhabiting a certain body that thinks, feels, and performs actions that attempt to fill our most important needs. If we erroneously choose to perform an undesirable action, the problem lies in our faulty perception, not us. We are fine. It's our awareness that's off. Align awareness back with reality, with what's really going on, without the bias of how we are choosing to see it and the faulty perception disappears.

71

Acceptance of what has happened is the
first step to overcoming the consequence
of any misfortune. - William James

To love someone means to see him
as God intended him.
- Feodor Dostoevsky

We can't change the present moment, but we can choose to change the future by changing our perception of reality.

Think of someone you love. What makes that person who he is? His essence or personality, not his accomplishments. Whatever he has accomplished in life, no matter how important it may be, does not make him who he is. You don't love someone because of a certain achievement. You love him because of the kind of person he is that would cause him to perform that kind of action. Without these accomplishments, he is still the same person. While you are not your actions, you are responsible for them and their consequences.

Everything you do causes a consequential result
from which you either benefit or suffer
and it's all by your choice.

No one is to be blamed for what he does. You do *only* what you *can* do at any given time. You evaluate all the information your awareness feeds you and weigh it against your highest priority. At any given time, no matter what, you will have only one choice... and that is what you will invariably choose to do. You have no other options possible at that precise moment of time based on the facts as you presently know them.

One evening I was making reservations for a flight to the East coast. I had found several possibilities that would work, but couldn't quite make up my mind what days and time would work best. Using online booking I found the best fare possible and was ready to buy, when my ego-voice interrupted me to be *sure* I had the best choice before I clicked. While I sat there arguing with myself the screen timed out, so when I did click to buy the screen said it couldn't process my request. By the time I did my search again, the fare was gone. Frantic, I found a second choice slightly higher. Clicked to buy... sold out. In just minutes the price had jumped fifty dollars. I searched again, quickly rearranging my criteria of how early I wanted to leave. Found a third choice, clicked to buy and was happy to have it at last – even though the price was higher than I wanted. I had gone from being fussy about departure times and cheapest rates, to end up paying more and

There is no heavier burden
than a great potential.
- Charlie Brown

There is never
a time and place
when we are powerless.
There are merely times we
forget
who we truly are.
- Doreen Virtue

leaving less conveniently, to finally being happy to be going before it was even more expensive or worse, sold out at any price.

At any given moment, all your options narrow down to one.

That is the choice you will make.

At that moment of choice, if you could instantly change your heredity, your instincts, or your life experiences, you would have different options open to you. But you can't change them in an instant. They are what they are. Based on that information, you make your only possible choice. It is the best that you can do at that moment of time, given that information and how you see it.

You are the only one capable of making your own choices in life. And you are responsible for the outcome of your choices. Live consciously, aware of your choices.

Any aspects of reality in which it appears you have had no choice,

was preceded by a moment in which you *did* have a choice.

Thus, you cannot be a victim of circumstances when you are in fact the creator of the circumstances. If you will take responsibility for your apparent lack of positive things in your life, you will be empowered to consciously change that. By taking responsibility for what you have generated in your life, you will manifest what you desire.

You do not forget or deny the facts. The facts are the facts. The truth is the truth. You are being who you are, conditioned by what you have been through, while doing the best you can from your own perspective.

It's all relative. It's all in how you see it through your own personal filters of your own perspective.

What does not kill me,
makes me stronger.
- Nietzsche,
Twilight of the Idols

A truly happy person is one who can enjoy the scenery on a detour.

It was a good idea at the time.

Chapter 6

Look for the Silver Lining

*A*s it is, reality is neither good nor bad by itself. It is our perception that determines whether we see something as negative or positive. If we let reality just *be*, removing all factors of good/bad, it no longer affects us. Many things happen in this world. Some directly affect our lives creating emotional ties. Others we don't take personally so they have no effect on us. More things happen that don't affect us, than do. Sometimes we create emotional bonds with situations about which we can do nothing.

It is only when we label something as good/bad

that we take it personally and give it the power to affect us.

When an unwanted event happens, no matter how much you want to change it, you can't. By choosing to see it as bad, you can create an emotional tie to the situation. The strength of the tie will determine how upset you can be. Feeling bad is naturally destructive. Instead look for something positive to come out of it, even just a lesson learned the hard way. That is your key to finding the silver lining. Otherwise, the only thing you will accomplish is to be upset while whatever happened goes unchanged, because you can't change it. You may be able to find a way to not have it happen again,

Remember Pollyanna and her cloying determination
to find the good in any situation.
- Sarah Ban Breathnach, *Simple Abundance*

Let the adversity go,
keep the experience.

but you can't alter the reality that it has already happened. Sometimes the only silver lining you can find is a lesson learned.

In 1913, Eleanor H. Porter gave us a lasting concept: Pollyanna and her Glad Game. Seriously ill with few material possessions and unsupported emotionally, the creative mind of this child teaches us to cope with adversity by finding within it reasons to be grateful. If you find that too difficult, then at least dissolve as many emotional bonds as possible. Less emotion equals more peace.

Stop finding fault with the world around you.
It just is.

If you continue to find fault with reality, all you will do is make yourself miserable... and reality won't change. Your first mental action is to accept it. Your second step is to determine whether or not you can do something to rectify the situation. If you can, do it. If you can't, then go back to step one, accept it. Then let the experience and any resulting trauma go as soon as you are able. Otherwise, you open yourself to unhappiness. And for what purpose? You will be unhappy and reality will remain the same, except now you have doubled the impact of the negative event. You create more negativity by causing a second negative event, your emotional trauma. Now you are no longer happy. You will remain unhappy for as long as you choose to continue to feel that way. It is, after all, always your choice.

Not that you're supposed to feel joyous in a negative situation, attempting to deny that anything bad happened. Acknowledge instead that it is a negative event you can do nothing about, and end its power there. Assume a neutral emotional involvement. You can't change it, so agree it is not so good and you don't like it, and then let it go. Getting more upset only hurts *you* and you're already hurting after taking on this emotional injury.

Let it happen without judgment.

How can you keep a positive attitude in the midst of negativity? Suspend judgment, allow it to be, and do not create any emotional bonds. Rather than wasting energy arguing and refusing to accept it, you can agree to accept it *as is*, and

It is the greatest of all mistakes to do
nothing
because you can only do a little.
Do what you can.
- Sydney Smith

Ultimately,
time is all you have and
the idea isn't to save it,
but to savor it.
- Ellen Goodman

direct your energy towards positive ends, possible solutions, and sound self esteem. The only way to consistently do this is by remembering events outside of you have no effect on your self esteem.

Know your Self, care for your Self, judge not your Self, and consequently feel so good about yourself that you no longer need to find fault and want to change a reality you can do nothing about. Our natural state is to feel positive, by being positive and generating good will.

By deciding something is bad and letting it get to us, we lose our natural state of being positive.

Sometimes we form conclusions without realizing that our awareness is faulty. The decision we make will therefore be faulty, our reaction incorrect. We'll wish later that it were otherwise. Life on earth is a learning experience for us. We're perfect spirits sometimes making regrettable decisions. None of that makes us bad. It is how we learn.

Any negative actions, thoughts, feelings, that you generate are not a part of your inner self, the essence that inhabits the human physical part of you and makes you alive. That essence does not age, even while your body does, and is inherently good.

Adversity happens.

Let's say you're driving in your car and someone cuts in front of you, and then slows down. You're in a hurry. You're late, and the car in front of you isn't even doing the speed limit now. You have several choices. You can decide you simply are not going to let it bother you. People are people and some people have no idea what they are doing at any given time. Or you can get angry and escalate from there as each passing moment makes you later. If you have chosen the latter reaction, once the incident is over you have two choices once again. You can choose to calm down and let it go out of your consciousness, or you can choose to maintain that anger. You can hang on to it and draw as much negative energy from it as possible right into yourself. You can go through your memory banks and dig up every similar situation you can remember and build that negativity into a super power that controls your life. The more negative energy you

Do your best.
Then, don't worry, be happy.
- Meher Baba

When you are in harmony with life and love,
you always win,
although you might not always get
what you mistakenly think you ought to have.
- Terry Cole-Whittaker,
What You Think of Me Is None of My Business

generate, the more you hurt yourself. Yet no matter how much pain you choose to create for yourself, reality will still not change for you.

Since you can't alter reality, to create necessary change, you must revise your perception of it somehow. Your perception of reality cannot be different unless the input is different.

Your particular perception of reality is formed by your heredity, natural instincts, and your interactions with this world. You can't change your heredity, or the natural feelings and instincts you were born with that make you who you are. You can change only one thing – your interaction with the world around you.

Alter how you interact and the equation changes, and alters your perception of reality. This new input allows for different awareness and therefore different results.

There is never any reason for putting yourself down, for any loss of self esteem.

At any given moment you are doing the best that you are capable of doing. Even if it's a poor job and you know you've done better at other times. At that precise moment due to whatever contributing factors are going on (you feel tired, ill, angry, depressed, etc.) you are still doing the best you can do. Don't beat yourself up for it. Let it go. Decide to do better the next time.

Alter the equation and get a different result.

Even just that simple thought acknowledging that you know you could do better is enough. We will always do the only thing we can do. After all options are weighed, only one is left and that's our choice because we would rather not do the alternative or have the alternative happen.

For instance, say you stay up late one night. The next morning when your alarm rings, you're exhausted. You'd rather stay in bed and sleep. You consider the possibilities of doing this. If you choose to sleep, you'll be late for work. Showing up that late for work increases the probability of being fired. To avoid this happening, you must get up. Or,

Experience is a
hard teacher
because she
gives the test
first, the lesson
afterwards.

We never shall have any more time.
We have, and will always have,
all the time there is.
- Arnold Bennett

you could sleep just a few minutes — you feel any little bit would be most welcome — by hitting the snooze alarm. But you know that even that small change would still make you late enough to be reprimanded. What to choose?

You'll make your choice based on what you want to avoid the most as well as the result you prefer. Sleep, snooze, be late, or give up and get up — you determine what is most important to you and that will be your only possible choice. No matter how many different ways you examine the situation, what you choose will be the only choice you can make. Your choice is simply based on which action will produce the result that you feel is the most important.

It is impossible to try harder
because you are already doing your best -
whatever that looks like.

You can't do better by trying harder. You must change the input, alter the equation, and then your actions can be different. It would seem like you are doing better because you are trying harder. In actuality you changed a factor and now your best is different from before.

Say you're holding a wrench on a handle and it won't turn. You can't try harder. You're already exerting all the strength you have. Someone comes by and shows you a different way to place the wrench on the handle so that you have better leverage. Now your best makes the handle turn. Your best improved because the equation changed, not because you tried harder. New information provided new input. With the new data, you are now able to do better because the equation's different.

Change how you perceive life
and your life will change accordingly.

Any fault you find with reality, any problem you have with it, disappears the instant you change your perspective or your perception.

> There is no happiness
> where there is no wisdom.
> - Sophocles

> We know the truth, not only
> by the reason, but by the heart.
> - Blaise Pascal

No matter how bad you feel any situation is, look for the silver lining. If it isn't obvious, you may have to search for it, but it's always there. Some things are simply harder to find or figure out than others.

Remember the concept of the Glad Game and simply be grateful. You would not be exactly who you are right now without having had every single incident in your life happen to you. If any one thing had not happened as it did, you would not be the same person you are today. Each experience counts and each reaction to the experience is important.

Should you find it difficult to be grateful for the person you are today, then don't you think it's time to change? Change how you feel about the past. Change your future reactions. You have that power within you. The time to begin is now.

This above all. To thine own self be true,
and it must follow as the night the day,
thou canst not be false to any man.
- Shakespeare

As he thinketh in his heart, so is he.
- Proverbs 23:7

You don't give up the intention,
and you don't give up the desire.
You give up your attachment to the result.
- Deepak Chopra

Chapter 7

It's About Responsibility

Where Do You Get It?

*F*or every choice we make, whether we choose to do it or not do it, we are responsible. *Even not making a choice, is a choice.* We will inevitably benefit from or suffer the consequences for these choices. If we are going to benefit or suffer for our choices and have full responsibility for them, the smartest thing to do is to consciously take charge of our lives.

The only way to take charge of your life

is to use your Inner Authority

to determine your belief system and values.

No one else can determine your belief system for you. Others can make recommendations, but remember their recommendations are based on *their* belief system which may not have the same values as yours. You were born with your own Inner Authority. You *know* when something is right. You can feel it inside of you. Your Inner Authority is what gives you that knowing. It's your intuition and it determines your values and gives you your belief system.

*The diamond cannot be polished
without friction,
nor the man perfected
without trials.
- Chinese Proverb*

Every beginning is a consequence.
Every beginning ends something.
- Paul Valery, French Poet

We can do only
what it is that we have decided to do.

Each of us must be constantly aware of our thoughts and allow only those that are in line with our belief system if we want to be in conscious control of our lives. We pay a price for everything we do. Every choice carries a price. The price is the consequence of our chosen action. The greater our awareness, the better we are able to evaluate the projected consequences.

Yet we allow how others treat us to determine how we will feel.

You can start out the day in a good mood, then have a problem with someone at home and have it "ruin your day." You can be feeling fine, and then spend the day at work with a boss who decides to take a bad mood out on you. In either situation, it is you who decides just how much you will allow someone else to have power over how you will feel. Good self esteem gives you the inner security to hold on to feeling good no matter what you experience at another's whim.

We depend on someone else to realize what our needs are
and expect our needs to be met,
even though no one else has any way of knowing what they are.

When we meet new people and discover we like them, it's usually because we find we have a great deal in common — thinking alike and feeling the same way about many things. This leads us to consequently make the false assumption that they will automatically know what we need, and supply that need. When they fail to do that, we get upset with them because they have fallen short of our expectations. Yet they are not liable for their failure because there was no way they could have known what it was that we expected them to do for us.

No matter what hindsight may show to be the better choice, at the specific moment of choosing, we cannot force ourselves to make a different choice. Our awareness at that moment always limits us to one choice only. Nothing can make us choose anything else.

I never give them hell.
 I just tell the truth and they think it's hell.
- Harry S. Truman

Never answer an
anonymous letter.
- Yogi Berra

Only when we receive new input is change possible for a different choice. You are always free to choose anything within your capabilities to do, but not without paying the price demanded. You have the authority to choose, the innate right and freedom to act in a destructive and immoral manner, but you are responsible and you will pay the price for doing so.

Everyday you can choose to feel good or to feel bad.

It's a choice you have to make. Staying in the positive means not making decisions as to whether something is good or bad, and just letting reality be without the omnipresent label. Take any event, label it bad, get upset, and there goes feeling good right out of your awareness. You have just stepped on the negative path.

An unwanted event cannot be changed, only dealt with. You can only choose your reaction to it, nothing more. The event won't change or disappear just because you feel really, really bad. It will still be the same but now you're miserable. Or you can choose to accept the reality – which will exist anyway – and continue to feel okay. It doesn't mean you now like the unwanted situation that you can't change. It does mean you are willing to let it be, give it no attention. More important, you haven't given it power over you.

It means not making it personal. Let reality be without emotional attachment.

Let's say you make plans to go to the movies with a friend. An hour before you're due to meet, the friend calls to cancel because another friend called with something better to do. This makes you feel *worth-less*, i.e. worth less than whatever it is that was chosen over you. You were feeling good about the plans you had. Now they are gone and naturally you're upset by the turn of events. You can either let it ruin your day, or choose to accept the situation and let it go without fussing about it. You can choose to be angry with the friend, tell him how you feel and even consider terminating your friendship, or you can simply realize that this friend is not reliable. Accept him for the type of person he is and consequently how he is capable of treating others, and learn from the experience. Accept

The Power that created you is the Power
that works through you.
You have the equipment
to live life.
You have the ability
to change your mind.
- Raymond Charles Barker,
How to be Healthy, Wealthy, Happy

You can love other people only
to the degree that you've come
to love and accept yourself.
- Shakti Gawain

the feelings you have, but don't let them control you. You can choose to remain friends with the person or not, but it is necessary to forgive him. Forgiveness does not pardon unacceptable behavior. It does free yourself from the hurt. If you hang onto the anger and pain, it can make you sick. You can move on with your life only when you release the hurt. Holding resentment against someone, binds you to the person, the emotion, and the incident. It gives both the person and the incident power over you. You don't need it.

The only way to achieve sound self esteem is to realize and accept your own value.

You have inherent worth just as you are. When you allow yourself to love and respect your Self, giving your Self the same value as someone you value and love, only then will you be able to accept love and be loved by another. If you feel you have no value, then you surround yourself with people and things and circumstances that support and perpetuate that belief. You will feel worthless and be able to prove it by just looking around you. All you need is a decision to change it, and piece by piece, you can rebuild your self esteem with every choice you make.

Living a Conscious Life is to be aware of what is going on *with* you and *around* you.

What you desire is what will motivate you. When you decide to change what motivates you, you change the result. Your behavior can change only when you are motivated by a changed perception of reality.

Get a different perspective.

Perceive reality differently. It will change how you see things, as well as your reactions. If you want to change your life, you have to change your attitude. The way to change your attitude is to change your perspective of any situation. And the way to do that is to be aware, live a conscious way of life. You can no longer afford to be asleep at the wheel. The time for sleeping is over.

Nobody can be you as efficiently
as you can.
- Norman Vincent Peale

Always remember you're unique.
Just like everyone else.

A man's true wealth is the good he does in the world.
- Mohammed

Chapter 8

Intrinsic Value

Value by Default

*Y*our worth is innate. Everything in existence has value. Even though we sometimes call things worthless, they really aren't. That's the reason Thrift Stores have become big business. One person's junk is the answer to someone else's need. That means everything has value to someone for no other reason than it exists in reality. If it's here, there's a reason for it, and it has value by default. Subsequently, you're here so you have built-in value that doesn't have to be proved.

You are unique. There is no one else like you. Not one other person in this entire universe has your exact heredity, instincts and experiences, not even someone else in your family. Siblings can have very different experiences with their own parents.

Everyone is doing the best that they can

based on how they perceive reality.

The best that you can do at any time is based on your perspective. How many times have you said, "If I would have known...". After the fact, you realize that had you different information, or looked at it another way, you would have chosen differently and gotten a much different result. One which you would have liked better than what you received.

Overcoming negative self-image is
the first step in taking
responsibility for self.
- Dr. Barbara King,
Transform Your Life

Your own will come to you.
- Joel Goldsmith

A human tendency is for us

to constantly compare ourselves to others.

Comparing yourself to someone else to determine your own value is illogical. It is possible to compare the traits of two people by listing their attributes. Whether they have anything in common or not, one doesn't have any more value than the other. They can be totally different, yet they have equal worth. One may be better suited than the other for a certain function, but that does not make one better than the other, just different. If you're building a house, you need a carpenter. If your car breaks down, you need a mechanic. Each profession has equal purpose and value although what they accomplish is totally different.

We each have our own talents and abilities. Your talents are what comes easy for you. You may be a great cook, but helpless at designing an office plan. Therefore, you consult a designer when you need one and don't feel bad about doing so. Maybe the consultant can't cook. You are both equally valuable, but comparing your culinary expertise with another's design capabilities doesn't make any sense.

Our choices are based on whatever it is

that we think will make us feel good.

Our desires respond to our predominate need motivating us to do what we do. Everyone wants to feel good. Even a selfless act is impossible because the end result of our choice is to make ourselves feel good. When a person selflessly sacrifices himself for a greater good, that choice was made because the decision made that person feel good, first and foremost, even if it takes his life.

Sometimes of course we can be very wrong in what we think makes us feel good. What may appear on the surface to be a very good idea, when executed, fails to bring the desired result. Then we're not so happy.

Your slant on how you perceive reality,

determines your reaction to it.

The universe is change;
our life is what our thoughts make it.
- Marcus Aurelius

The price of greatness is
responsibility.
- Winston Churchill

Your choices are limited by your awareness. Your decision is based on your heredity, instincts, and experiences which are unlike anyone else's. Actions, like everything else, are neutral until we judge and label them as a positive or negative consequence of a situation.

You can only do what you can do,

and it will be the best that you can do

because it's the only thing you can do.

Sometimes when you are doing something, your heart is just not in it for whatever reason. You're doing a terrible job and you can't make yourself care to do any better. You aren't doing your best and you know it. The reality is, that really *is* the best you can do at that moment. There are times that your best is simply terrible and there is nothing you can do about it, until you change one of the existing factors. You must change your attitude, change your energy level, or change how you are thinking to be able to change your mind and your actions that result.

If you broke your dominant hand, it would be difficult to sign your name. You could do the absolute best that you are able to do, but unless you are ambidextrous it would be a scribble and far cry from your usual best. Terrible, but the best you could do.

We value judge just about everything, issue labels of good, bad or indifferent, and thus determine whether we benefit or suffer from the consequences. We choose one action to avoid another we'd rather not have happen. We make our choices, and become responsible for them. We are free to choose among all potential possibilities, but we cannot escape responsibility for every thought, word and deed.

Needs are stronger than knowledge. Our dominating needs will get us to do whatever it is we have to do to fulfill those needs. Even when we know better, we will ignore that information if it creates an obstacle to our satisfaction of fulfilling that predominating desire. This is when we say, "I knew better than to do that, but I just had to...." For instance, whenever we are late for an appointment it's because we chose to make something else be more important than being on time. Any excuse comes down to that. You will choose the most important thing for you to do, given how you feel about it.

Life can be found only in the present moment.
The past is gone, the future is not yet here…
- Thich Nhat Hanh, *For the Love of God*

When you surrender to what is and so become fully present, the past ceases to have any power.
- Eckhart Tolle, *Practicing the Power of Now*

Remove emotional attachment and any judgmental labels of good, bad, fair, unfair, become merely descriptive, like red or yellow. Any action is a reaction to something else. Actions are neutral until we label them. These labels can just be descriptive, or they can provoke an emotional response. Often we describe things by comparison to something else, and sometimes we use certain words just to evoke that emotional response.

When you look at your past,

realize every choice was made because

it was the only thing you could do.

Based on your preferences and your desire to avoid or precipitate a certain outcome, you made a choice. It became your choice because it was the only choice that would result in the desired outcome. Thus, it became the *only* thing you could choose. Any other choice would have negated the particular result you were looking for.

Judging yourself for any mistakes you may have made, assuming blame and guilt for them, is a waste of time. It happened. It's over. Take the lesson and let it go. "Why did you do that?" Because it was the *only* thing you *could* do. No other choice was possible because you felt any other choice would have failed to give you the desired outcome, right or wrong. Don't judge yourself and don't accept anyone else's judgment of you. It was the best that you could do because of how you thought and felt and what you wanted at that moment, even if it didn't always turn out exactly like you thought it would. Fault is found in the reasoning, not in you.

When we get upset with someone,

it is because we have equated the identity of that person

with their faulty reasoning and actions.

Once we have merged that person's identity with their actions, we can proceed with judgment and condemnation. While we are all responsible for our actions, all blame does is erode someone's self esteem and solves nothing. Looking to cast blame is time wasted that would have been better spent on finding a solution. Often many people find themselves locked into the blame syndrome unable to even think about a solution.

Toward those whom we see in
what we think of as sin,
our attitude must always be one of forgiveness,
not of forgiving them as much as forgiving ourselves
for seeing them erroneously.
- Joel Goldsmith,
The Attitude of Prayer

*We each need to make peace
with our own memories.
We have all done things
that make us flinch.*
- Lama Surya Das

The way to stop value judging is to change your perception of reality, and remove emotional attachment. In other words, you have got to change how you see things. If you can look at it another way, you can continue to feel good. You deserve to feel good because you have worth. Feeling bad accomplishes nothing positive. It doesn't change what happened or alter the circumstances in any way. You just emotionally involve yourself needlessly to the possible detriment of your self esteem.

Even if you don't believe it, you *are* in control of how you feel.

We will feel good until we decide to judge something not good, and want it to be otherwise when it cannot be. We determine whether or not we will feel bad about it, and for how long we will allow ourselves to feel bad. The more we can avoid a judgmental attitude in all its forms, the happier we will be. We cause our own pain. Everyone has bits and pieces of reality they don't want in their life, but it is the emotional attachment to them that causes us to be upset.

When you read in the news that another celebrity marriage is up for divorce, you might feel sympathy or you might feel nothing and just think it's a shame. Usually, however, the news wouldn't upset you the same way it would if it was happening to you. The difference is the amount of emotional involvement. Emotional attachment tends to pass judgment on the situation, determine it not to be good, and the result is you get upset. You cannot change the situation, yet if you can manage to change how you feel about it, you can go back to feeling good and end feeling bad. Better choice, yes?

The surest way to be hurt is to have expectations that won't or can't be met.

We become vulnerable when we depend on fulfillment of our needs by that which we do not have control over. Whether or not we feel good is then determined by how well our expectations are fulfilled. Having no control over any factors outside of us, we simply open ourselves to vulnerability.

Knowing others is wisdom.
Knowing the self is enlightenment.
- Lao Tzu,
Tao Te Ching

I don't need you to tell me I'm okay.

I know I'm okay.

Just as I am.

Let's say you make a new friend. You're excited to have lunch with her. Then she cancels. You can be disappointed, but will you let it ruin your entire day? You make some outdoor plans. It rains, so you can't go. How upset do you become when you can't have your way? You look for approval from a family member or friend and fail to get it. In fact, you're put down and made to feel like a loser. How much effect do you let this have on you?

When you recognize your own worth and know that you have value,

nothing anyone can say or do to you

will have any affect on your self esteem.

If someone calls you "stupid" or has a tone of voice that puts you down because your actions weren't quite right, that's hard to accept and feel okay. Your self esteem must be strong to counteract that opinion. If you failed to perform some act correctly, that does not make you stupid. Inept, perhaps. Stupid only if you continue to perform that same action getting the same unwanted results. Then you would have to consider why you are doing that and take responsibility for your actions.

Or if someone should say you are fat, true or not, that could be considered insulting and shake your self esteem tree. If it is a false statement and meant simply to be insulting, then that opinion does not matter. If it is true, then it is a statement of fact – like the sky is blue. A statement of fact is a statement of reality. So what? And your point was? Let it mean as little as that. If you don't take the insult, it can't hurt you. Let the giver hold the snapping turtle and he will get bit instead of you.

With high self esteem comes security and humility because you know your value is not affected by the opinions of others. Your feelings can always be hurt. Your self esteem can be affected only if *how* you see yourself is determined by someone other than yourself. You know the truth of your worth and, if there are those whose opinion of you tries to diminish you in any way, it doesn't matter. That's their opinion and they are entitled to it, even when you feel it's wrong. Their erroneous opinion may hurt your feelings but can't hurt your self esteem when *you* know you're okay.

Everyone is entitled their opinion, even when it's wrong.

We ourselves feel that what we are doing is
just a drop in the ocean.
But if that drop was not in the ocean,
I think that ocean will be less
because of that missing drop.
- Mother Theresa

Good judgment comes from bad experience,
and a lot of that comes from bad judgment.

We all like to engage in criticism at some time. It's hard not to since we each think our opinion is right. Whether it's friends, family, or strangers offering their opinions, if it is simply critical and not correcting, it is needless and unkind. Criticism is a good idea when it encourages change. In order for a different choice to be available, our perception of reality must be sufficiently altered. Blaming someone for an outcome just to lay out a guilt trip is cruel and pointless. Guiding someone to see a different viewpoint accomplishes growth and change.

Jane and Chet were moving to another state. Chet went first to get a job and Jane stayed to pack up their house. While Jane was talking to her sister she mentioned that moving was going to cost them almost $7000. Her sister, Lorraine, asked why Jane wasn't renting a truck and doing the moving herself. Jane replied it was too much to do. Lorraine said that when she moved two girlfriends helped her load the truck and drive it two states over. She had heard Jane say she was worried about money, yet here she was hiring a moving company. Lorraine was aggravated that Jane was so foolish spending money she didn't have. Jane heard the irritation in her voice which started her reconsidering. Later she mentioned to Lorraine that she'd talked to a friend who owned a moving van and was willing to drive it for her as well as another couple of friends who offered to help her pack and load the truck. Through Lorraine's criticism of her decision, Jane was able to see a different viewpoint she didn't see before.

Whatever our unique brand of reasoning is, it is all we have.

Each of us has only one available choice at the moment of decision – to do what our awareness tells us to do. We can't be angry with others, or resent them, when we fully accept the reality that all of our actions are the only choices possible for us. When we choose to live a conscious life, we are more apt to be aware of the consequences of our choices and take responsibility for them.

Compared to the universe, you are an infinitesimal part, yet you are of significance because each of us is unique. There is no one else that is exactly the same as you. Therefore, no one else can have the same impact on the world as you do. If you decide

> *Let us train our minds to desire what the situation demands.*
> *- Seneca, Moral Essays*

A closed mouth gathers no foot.

to sit it out, failing to perform your life's purpose, it *will* make a difference. It is very important what you choose to do. Choose wisely.

Every action has meaning and purpose
and results in a reaction.

The point is to learn and grow from your experiences, both pleasant and not so pleasant. Love yourself for you have value and treat others with the same respect. The more secure your self esteem is the better you are able to treat others, and the less it matters what others think.

There are two ways to live your life.
One is as though nothing is a miracle,
the other is as though everything is a miracle.
- Albert Einstein

In order to transform others,
you first must transform yourself.
- Mahatma Gandhi

Surrender is the simple but profound wisdom of
yielding to rather than opposing the flow of life.
- Eckhart Tolle, *The Power of Now*

Chapter 9

CYA

Change Your Attitude

*U*nwanted realities are caused by ourselves, others, and events that happen to us. Resistance is arguing with what is. It is the refusal to accept that which we do not have the power to change or that we are not willing to pay the price to change. There are things that will not and cannot change no matter how much we argue with ourselves over them. All negativity, unhappiness, and suffering come from resistance. To quote the Borg from Star Trek, "Resistance is futile." To surrender is to accept what is.

When those close to us die, no matter how upset we are, no amount of tears will bring them back. We can try to deny it. We can wish it were different. We can call it by another name, but the reality of that death will remain. You can't change a negative reality. All you can do is to stop resisting it. Accept what has happened and then change your attitude about it.

When you can change reality, do it.

When you can't, change your attitude.

Don't take guilt trips.
Take a trip to the mall,
to the next county,
to a foreign country,
but NOT to where
the guilt is.

The finest qualities of our nature,
like the bloom on fruits, can be
preserved only by the most
delicate handling. Yet we do not
treat ourselves nor one another
thus tenderly.
- Henry David Thoreau, *Walden*

If you don't like where you live, but are unwilling to go through the process of finding a new home and the turmoil of moving, then that says you consider the price too high to change your circumstances. You must then accept, make peace with what you have, and let the thought of change go.

We can be our own worst enemy. We can go from feeling good to feeling bad because of our own thoughts. That little voice in our heads that's ready at a second's notice to criticize us. The moment we perceive something we have done is not up to some standard we have set for ourselves, we immediately place a negative value judgment on our own heads. Most of us don't even need someone else to put us down. We have already done a much better job on ourselves then anyone else could ever do. Additional help in that area isn't needed, although it is often freely offered.

We identify with our faulty reasoning that resulted in the faulty action and label ourselves as *less than*.
Less than what we think we should be; less than everyone else.

Sound self esteem is maintained by not listening to that little voice, by remembering that no matter how badly we think we did, it was the absolute best that we could have done at that time.

Try this exercise: Go back to your childhood and think of a situation in which you acted badly. See yourself as that child and now imagine yourself as an adult standing next to your child-self in that situation. You see a child crying, upset over what happened. Would you let that child continue to cry or would you tell your child-self that it's okay, everyone makes mistakes?

As a child or as an adult, it is the same. Learn from your mistakes. Let the emotion go, and get on with the day, with the rest of your life. In other words, get over it. Carrying the baggage of a drama queen past won't help you or anyone else.

No matter how much you wish it were different,
you could not have done better than what you did.

Perspective vs perception:
Change your perspective and your perception changes.

I thought about the times I
feel a sense of struggle,
trying to force the universe
to behave the way I think it
should. Sooner or later, I
realize that I would rather
have peace.
- Alan Cohen,
Joy Is My Compass

Most of us fail to realize just how hard we are on ourselves with our negative monkey chatter. "You stupid... why did you do that... can't you ever stop and think first... of all the dumb things to do... can't you ever do anything right... for once in your life could you..." We abuse ourselves without realizing what we are saying, without thinking of the consequences. If others said the same things to us, we would be outraged saying, "how dare you" and most likely demand an apology from them.

To be able to achieve a different result, you have to alter your perception of reality, change the information you are using. You are responsible for what you do and you will inevitably benefit or suffer from the consequences whatever they are, but you do not gain or lose any value in the transaction. Your worth as an individual remains unchanged. Your awareness must acknowledge and accept this as fact.

As an alternative to putting ourselves down, we frequently give others the power and permission to upset us. We do this when we either allow their opinion of us to matter more than our own opinion does, or when we feel they have not met our own personal standard of conduct.

We give others power over us to determine

whether or not we will feel good,

when we place a value on their actions.

Jim made and sold birdhouses at the local flea market. An owner of a store in town liked his work and gave him a large order for a special promotion.

Jim accepted the order but realized he needed help to get them done in time. When Jim told Steve about the jam he was in, his friend offered to build half of them. Steve said he'd been making birdhouses himself, giving them away as presents. He seemed confident and Jim recalled that Steve had always been good at woodworking, so he agreed. He showed Steve the various styles, gave him instructions and materials as well as the delivery date he needed them.

Two weeks later Steve showed up, proudly showing off his completed birdhouses. Jim examined one and was totally amazed. The workmanship was terrible. The wood cuts

> *We are disturbed not by things but the views that we take of things.*
> *- Epictetus, The Enchiridion*

We shall be made truly wise if we be made content, not only with what we can understand, but content with what we do not understand...
- Charles Kingsley

were still rough, not finished. The front entry hole was off center from the peak of the roof. The painting was sloppy. The work was poorly done and yet Steve seemed proud of it. Jim realized too late that Steve was not the craftsman he pretended to be. He was ashamed to add Steve's work to his own. Jim went from the elation of a completed job, to shock, to anger. He had relied on Steve, who had no idea that his work was unacceptable. Jim had expected to be celebrating. Instead, he vacillated between depression and anger. Jim couldn't help but feel that Steve was worthless. Steve had failed him and almost ruined his business. It seemed that every time he tried to trust others to do something right, it always turned out wrong.

It is only when we have decided that our standard of values have not been met that our emotions turn negative. They have failed us and now we feel bad. We judge and form a negative response for an invalid reason. We forget they too have done their very best, no matter how bad a job we think that was, and are not the less for having done it poorly.

With sound self esteem we no longer find it necessary
to place a value judgment on another.

When you feel good about yourself, you will find that you can remove all emotional attachment and let reality be. Actions are what they are, and it's okay. When you have high self esteem, you would no sooner judge another, than you would judge yourself. Everyone is always doing the best that they can at any given moment.

Find a way to think of it in a positive way
and it will no longer have negative power over you.

Events created by ourselves and others comprise the third area of our lives that can upset us. Any event, situation, or condition that we wish were otherwise when we cannot control it or change it, can cause us to feel bad. When we cannot change the event, all we can change is our attitude towards it. While I'm certainly not saying that is easy to do, it is necessary if you wish to maintain your peace of mind and not get yourself caught in a downward spiral. Letting something have power over you will seldom help you.

> Life is the movie you see
> through your own eyes.
> It makes little difference
> what's happening out there.
> It's how you take it that
> counts.
> - Denis Waitley

> The grand essentials to happiness in this life
> are something to do, something to love,
> and something to hope for.
> - Joseph Addison

With sound self esteem, you feel positive about yourself in every way. You no longer find it necessary to find fault with realities that you can not change. If you can do nothing about it, remove the emotional attachment and let the issue go as quickly as you can. Accept that your unwillingness to just let it be without value judgment is the problem, not the event. It does not have any power unless you make it so.

CYA in Action

1. When you find yourself beginning the cycle of placing a value judgment, or labeling something bad, STOP!

2. Remember it is neither good nor bad. It's your attitude, how you perceive it, that makes it bad. It is your ability to value judge that's caused a negative condition. Reality simply is and cannot be otherwise.

3. Realize that it can't have the power to affect how you feel unless you give it that power.

4. Realize that no matter how bad you feel, nothing will change. You're just compounding the misery by letting it affect you. If you maintain emotional attachment to it, you will continue to be upset.

5. If you can change it, do so. If you can't, let it go. Hurting won't make the situation better. It just hurts you.

Innumerable options are open to everyone all the time,
but are relatively infrequently chosen...
One's range of choice is ordinarily limited by one's vision.
- David Hawkins,
Power vs. Force

Nothing is sadder than to die with your
music still buried inside of you.
- Rosita Perez, *The Music Is You*

You fulfill the promise that lies latent within you
by keeping your promises to yourself.
- David Harold Fink

Chapter 10

It's All About Choice

*Y*esterday ended last night. It's history. It cannot be changed. Tomorrow, yet to come, is a mystery full of choices. Today is a gift. That's the reason we call it the Present. Each morning is a blank slate, another chance to begin again. Our potential has no limits except those we choose by each thought, each word, and every thing that we do.

Each day we build our life choice by choice.

If we don't like what we have,

we can change our choices and have a different result.

Each of us has free will and the power of choice. What is it that we are free to do? Physically, we have bodies that we can care for or not. We can be anywhere on the spectrum from obsession with body care to unkempt and unfit. Mentally, we each have a mind we can fill with knowledge or choose to let it remain ignorant. We can choose to be positive or negative in our thinking. We can choose to be happy or not. This freedom to choose how and what we will become is our greatest freedom, the freedom of choice.

While you are studying this material, you will be exposed to many new concepts. They will remain concepts unless they become part of your thought process. The important ideas that are presented to you regarding thinking, acting, and reacting, will feel new and

There can be change without progress,
but not progress without change.

You're never too old
to grow younger.
- Mae West

quite often may contradict your old ways of doing things. They will continue to feel awkward until they replace your old habits. Once they become an automatic process, your life will expand in new directions.

Every situation gives us an opportunity to learn
and an opportunity to contribute something of value.

You've been making choices all your life. Some changes are sufficient unto themselves, and some beget further changes. It is never failure to stop where you are, turn around, and go in a different direction. That's as true when you are walking somewhere as when you make any choice in life.

Each day is a new beginning
and brings with it an opportunity for a new choice.

If you pick up a fork to eat dinner and then discover you're having soup, you don't insist on eating with a fork. No one would. You would change your utensil for a spoon. Yet often we stick with a poor decision we've made even though we know there is a better choice available.

Change is how we make progress.
To resist change is to miss opportunities.

What's the most prevalent reason that keeps us from making a change? Fear of failure, fear of mistakes. Yet to not try is admitting defeat before we've even begun.

If we don't try, we've already failed.
Mistakes are only lessons we need to learn.

Since our reasons for doing things exist only in our minds, we can always begin again and again, as often as we need to. There are no wrong choices. Each choice will simply bring a different experience. Each experience will bring a lesson and an opportunity to learn. When we are choosing, it is wisest to make our decision with as much information

Things do not change, we do.
- Henry David Thoreau

It must happen *in* us
before it can happen *to* us.
- Raymond Charles Barker, *Barkerisms*

as possible because some lessons are more costly than others. Some prices are so high, we would prefer not to have to pay them.

No matter what is going on in our lives, we can change it.

If you want to change something in your life, it is your thinking and attitude that must change first, not the outward appearance or the other person. It is possible to change your attitude in just minutes with an Attitude Adjustment Moment. There are two methods for doing this. Either one will redirect your energy to take you from the negative to the positive. One method is to use your Gratitude Stone and follow the exercise presented in Chapter 2. This process replaces the negative energy by recalling the good and giving thanks. The other method, the 2-AM tool, adjusts your attitude by redirecting your energy to a calm, peaceful place. When you use this method, you will quickly rid yourself of a negative experience and find yourself centered once more. The following exercise is the 2-AM tool.

Take a few deep breaths and still your mind. Take a few more deep breaths, exhale slowly and think of your favorite place. Your Shangri-La. The place where you'd rather be than here. The place you would go to if you wanted to get away from it all and feel safe, comfortable, happy. Picture yourself there now. Make as detailed a hologram as you can. Place there whatever you need to relax. Feel Good. Pull yourself back together again. Stay there for just a minute or two, more if you're inclined, 30 seconds if that's all you have. Pick up the energy of the place. Good, concentrated energy that will give you strength and a positive attitude again. You're okay. It's just the world around you that gets a little out of harmony sometimes and you get caught up in it. All of that is outside of you. You're fine. Feel centered, back in harmony. Take a few more deep breaths and resume your life. Whenever you need to feel calm and regain strength, go back there. Give it a name. Make it Your Place. It's the place to go to when life starts to get to you.

When you change your thinking,
your life will change accordingly, correspondingly.

Everyone has a mental image of themselves that they think comprises them, even though it is most likely composed of likes and dislikes that we form moment by moment.

Insanity: doing the same thing over and over again
and expecting different results.
- Albert Einstein

When an old pattern reappears...
this is the time to be very patient
with ourselves. Patience is an
affirmation of self-love.
- Gloria Karpinski,
Where Two Worlds Touch

We forget these are actually just our preferences and have no more importance or relevance than that. When you get caught up too deeply in your preferences, you end up thinking that is who you are. Not so. Your preferences, like the food you prefer, are true for the moment, but may have little to do with how you feel tomorrow. Realize what your preferences are and allow yourself to change them when necessary. This gives you the freedom to grow.

Even when you are open to change,

sometimes it is very difficult to release old thought patterns

and accept the new.

We tend to be biased based on our current belief system. A new choice necessarily means letting go of old beliefs. Often this is easier in theory than in practice. Without realizing it, we resist change because the old is more comfortable. Holding onto old beliefs, however, makes us resistant to change and growth, even when the old ways no longer work for us. We recreate the same patterns over and over. Too easily we form habits because of our repetitive thoughts and behaviors. Take a look at your life and make a decision to let go of that which is limiting.

Times change. People change. Already this 21st century is vastly different than the beginnings of the 20th century. We have to learn how to cope with things differently. Each of us must change too if we want new things to happen in our lives.

Albert Einstein stated that one definition of insanity is to continue doing the same things and expect different results. For different results to be possible, different actions and thoughts must be in place first.

We often do this in relationships. If the situation we are in turns bad, we tend to think of past relationships. Ones that we thought were good, pointedly ignoring the bad in them. We remember so and so, how wonderful it was to be with that person. Maybe we should go back and see about that relationship again. The important thing to remember is that there was a reason we stopped seeing that person. Most likely those reasons still exist. We will only discover that problem again if we choose to go down that same road.

All things are not only in a constant state of change, but they are the cause of constant and infinite change in other things.
- Marcus Aurelius

Our lives are shaped
not as much by our
experience as by our
expectations.
- George Bernard Shaw

The same goes for most situations. There was a reason something ended, be it living somewhere, a job, or spending time with someone. Whoever, whatever, unless the situation has changed so the reason no longer exists, the same problem that ended it in the first place will inevitably rise again. Unless of course, an element in the equation has changed. Then different input will equal a different result. Just realizing the possibility of a different result can alter the equation enough that we choose another course of action.

Change is inevitable and necessary
if the future is to be different from the past.

It seems to be part of human nature to want to control other people. We would like to control life. We demonstrate this when we resist accepting life the way it is, by wanting to look different than we do, or by insisting others behave differently. We tend to not be satisfied with the way we are. We tend to spend a great deal of time and energy wishing the world operated differently than it does.

We have the choice to be happy or not.

No matter what is happening around us, how we are going to feel about it is always a matter of choice. At times we feel like wishing for the "good old days," but you can't live in the past. Though it often feels like things never change, inexorably they do. They change enough that you can't go back to the past because you will find it to have become an illusion, no longer real. The biggest problem is that living in the past makes it impossible to create anything in the present.

Every moment with every choice
you create your life, every day.

Focusing on negatives will attract and generate more negative situations. The more you focus on the positive things you want, the more you will create positive situations in your life. We create more of whatever we give our attention to. Making the choice to live a conscious way of life means choosing to be awake and aware. All it takes is having conscious awareness of what our desires are and focusing our thoughts to that end. What

Don't let life discourage you.
Everyone who got where he is
had to begin where he was.
- Richard Evans

Repetition is a
convincing
argument.

we focus on, we will experience. Focus on something different and you will have different experiences.

If we live our life by the numbers, much like paint by numbers, we will continue to repeat and experience the same pattern, get the same outcome. Automated action produces repetitive results. The law of cause and effect always works. Whatever we think about, talk about, believe in, and dwell on is what will appear in our lives.

**We always have that choice to change our thinking
to change the conditions of our lives.**

Every door that may close on the left will open another door on the right through which we may pass to a greater world than we ever knew before.
- Christian Larson,
Pathway of Roses

...we often look so long and so regretfully at the closed door that we do not notice the one which has opened for us.
- Helen Keller

At last it dawned on me
that these obstacles were my life.
- Alfred D'Souza

Chapter 11

FAILURE -

as seen from a positive viewpoint

We all experience major changes in life. It's part of life's ongoing process. When you experience the loss of a job or a relationship, it's hard to believe that recovery is possible. It feels like the challenge is permanent. We're devastated by the loss, wonder what's wrong with us, where have we failed, focus on other failures, call ourselves incompetent. In general, we create and continue to generate an atmosphere of failure and feed it by dwelling on as many negatives as we can bring to mind.

**While many of these events can probably be life altering,
they also give us an opportunity for new choices and growth.**

As much as we would prefer to have them, the old choices are no longer available. That leaves us to set the limits of how much change we want to choose. A new way of life is open to us once we release the past.

**The only thing to do is to start over again, right where we are,
with whatever we have available.**

Success is not final,
failure is not fatal:
it is the courage to
continue that counts.
- Winston Churchill

We either make ourselves miserable,
or we make ourselves strong. The
amount of work is the same.
    - Carlos Castaneda

It's the same thing if we are using a GPS system. If we miss the turn it wanted us to take, the GPS simply reconfigures the route from where we are and begins again. So just as when we are traveling, we can reconfigure our lives whenever we choose, pick a new and different direction and head on over there.

It does not matter what the event was. Whether it was a relationship or situation, big or small, what you must do is the same. Basically, "Pick yourself up, dust yourself off, and start all over again." What does that mean? Rise above the situation, let go of what no longer works, make new choices, and begin again.

As difficult as this may seem at times, the alternative is even less attractive. You can succumb to the situation and let it get you down to the point of immobility, while you wait for someone to rescue you. This requires little effort on your part, and does not get you far. You can also extend even less effort on your own behalf and just give up without even waiting or wanting to be saved.

Frank wanted to start his own business. He had everything except money. He needed an investor. Frank told Jake about his situation. Jake thought it was a grand idea and said he knew someone who would be interested and had the money to invest. Jake would talk to Maurice. Maurice never called Frank. Frank then repeated the scenario with more friends. In each case, the person never had the money, but knew someone. However each potential investor never contacted Frank. He was ready to give up. He failed to realize that all of his choices were the same...a friend of a friend. A second hand referral just didn't work.

Sometimes we know there is a better choice
but we just don't choose it.

Our excuse is that we are waiting for things to be perfect. If we are truly honest with ourselves, we know that is just an excuse, a way of avoiding commitment and extending ourselves. Seldom will things be perfect. Make a decision to start now.

Failure is simply stopping
when the choice you made doesn't work.

When you discover you are riding a dead horse,
the best strategy is to dismount. - Dakota tribal wisdom

Fear is excitement without breath.
- Joseph Heller, *Bodywise*

Failure doesn't stop you. Failing to make another choice and trying again does. Not making a choice is a decision to do nothing. It is better to pick something, anything, rather than immobilization. Any choice is better than no choice at all. Successful people act on their choices and, if the results aren't what they had in mind, they reevaluate and choose again.

Frank was losing hope of ever starting his business. He expanded his search and tried banks and angel investors, but they declined the risk of a new venture. He surveyed his results. Friends, banks, and investors – none had come through. He had to face the reality that no one was going to help him. If he wanted his own business, he had to find a way to start it himself without outside investors. It was either that or stop where he was, and fail. Failure or success. It all depended on how much he wanted it and what he was willing to do to get it.

Start from where you are and go from there.

Gilbert Chesterton once wrote, "If a thing is worth doing, it is worth doing badly." What he was saying is that you can't wait until you are adept and skilled at something before attempting to do it, for you may never begin. Any mistakes are part of the journey and almost without exception, it is the journey that is of import, not the destination. Usually it is difficult to realize and accept that concept.

Your future is built on the choices you make today.

You can't control situations, but you can always control your reaction to life. You can move forward, or stay where you are and whimper about how unfair life is. You'll never know the limits of your potential unless you begin again and keep moving.

The only failure is to fall down and stay down.

When we do fall and admit defeat, we often create another stumbling block in our lives. Each time we can add another defeat to the stack around us until we feel unable to move. We can feel blocked in every direction, imprisoned by our failures and the choices we've made. We see it as failure, instead of seeing it as simply an impetus to change, an

Our greatest glory is not in never falling, but in rising every time we fall.
- Confucius

I couldn't repair your brakes,
so I made your horn louder.

opportunity to let go of that which no longer serves us. We can choose to see opportunity and challenge, or instead see another reason to quit.

Courage is not being without fear.

Should the road between where you are and where you want to be seem daunting, remember you are not doing it all at once. You don't have to have everything in place, figured out and planned beforehand. If you wait for the perfect time, you may never begin.

When I was just out of college and on my own I made a decision to drive from coast to coast, from California to Florida. I looked at the map seeing the three thousand miles between the two points. All I could think of was that I could never drive that distance alone. It was too much of an undertaking. The problem was that if I wanted to visit family, I had no other choice. I either had to find a way to get over this daunting distance factor, or agree to let it stop me. If I made a big deal out of it, it could paralyze me and I would never make the drive. This consequently meant that I also would fail to see my family. That was a big price to pay. Or, I could choose to down play it and find another way to look at the trip, which was the only way to get the result I most wanted. I decided to think of the distance in a different context. Instead of thinking of it as a trip of three thousand miles, I thought of it as a trip from simply point A to point B. The distance between these two points was the distance I was able to drive in one day. The first day I knew it would be easy to drive from sunrise to sunset. That would put me a third of the way. The next day, all I had to do was drive from B to C another single day's drive. That was very doable. The third day I'd be at my destination. If I thought of the total distance in smaller segments, it transformed the trip into three one-day trips that I could easily handle driving and did not find mentally daunting.

Courage is acknowledging your fear
and doing the thing you fear anyway.

141

> *Learn to let go,*
> *that is the key to happiness.*
> *- The Buddha*

In order to fly, you have to give up the ground you are standing on.
- Elia Wise, *Letter to Earth*

Be ALIVE while you are alive.

Chapter 12

Get Over It

$\mathcal{G}$etting over it, letting go, is not saying it was okay. It's about not involving your emotions, so you can separate yourself from whatever happened and let it be. Forgiving is not forgetting. It is not condoning. It is not soft. It is simply releasing anger, bitterness, and resentment so you can move on. If you don't, then you are choosing to allow your past to limit your future.

Sometimes we make the past greater than what it was. The past is no greater than the present. If we keep our attention on the past, it's like anchoring the future to what was. Just because the past was not what we desired, does not mean the future must be the same. In the present we can choose to continue the past or to let it go for a different future.

Part of life is experiencing loss and learning how to cope. This is as true with small things – the loss of your favorite pen, or your car, as with the larger things – the loss of a job, or a friendship, or the ultimate loss, the death of a loved one. We have to get over not having our way when we feel we simply must have it.

What ever it is, get over it and get on with your life. This may sound harsh, but this isn't the only lesson you have to learn. I often think that what we're supposed to learn is to *let go*. Everything around us is temporary although we tend to fool ourselves into

> *And when you have reached the mountaintop,*
> *then you shall begin to climb.*
> *- Kahlil Gibran*

> Your mind is the key to your experience, and your use of it determines your health, prosperity, and security.
> - Raymond Charles Barker, *Barkerisms*

thinking things will go on forever, just because it is what we want. The only thing permanent is the eternal energy of our spirits housed in these bodies. All else is transitory.

If you want to hang on to it, you are choosing to not get over it. If you choose to not get over it, then at least do something positive about it. Otherwise you're just whining and complaining... which means you need to get over it.

A lot of things that involve us are instances of wrong action. When correct action is ignored, an instance of evil has taken place. "Evil" is "live" backwards. That which is against life is bad; anything that is a reversal of life is evil. This is when we can choose to get involved to right a serious wrong. Collective energy is a powerful force that can cause changes. Activists for the environment, animal rights, or civil rights, turn the negative energy of abuse into the positive energy of reform.

You can't change the past.

The only necessary intrusion of the past into the present or future is the lesson you learned through the experience. You must be willing to let go of thoughts and ideas that no longer serve you. Letting go is not easy. Change is often difficult because it brings up the fear of the unknown. But there is no security in hanging on to what is no longer meaningful.

Sometimes you may feel like starting over in some area of your life. Starting over does not necessarily mean starting from scratch, or even changing anything you're doing now. It does mean changing your attitude and thinking. That is where you start. To take control of your life, to begin again in any area, you must consciously take control of your thoughts and feelings.

We need to make conscious choices to manifest the life that we want. In our 60,000 thoughts that we have every day, there's some combination of useless thoughts, fantasies, and productive thoughts. It's up to us to determine what our thoughts will accomplish. All that thinking means choices. Choices give us opportunities to grow, or we can choose an easier path and stay with what is familiar. In most instances no matter what the condition is, no matter how impossible it may appear, it is only an effect and we can change effects. The starting point of change is with our thoughts.

We do not become
happy because we
get what we want;
we get what we
want because we
choose happiness
first.
- Alan Cohen

It's but little good you'll do,
watering last year's crops.
- George Eliot

Be aware of what you are thinking. Every *thing* begins with a thought. Thoughts are energy. When you think life affirming thoughts, your life will be filled with positive energy. How you think determines how you live. Every day brings with it the promise of a new start in the adventure of life. The quality of the adventure begins with a thought. Your self esteem contains the power of creating the life you want for yourself. You are a very powerful person. You have the power to create the life that you most desire.

Think positive.

Focus on the good in the situation, in your life. It may take a great deal of searching to find it sometimes, but it is always there. If you can't seem to find it, keep looking. It *is* there. The idea is to keep moving forward, change your ways when change is indicated, but otherwise stop beating yourself up for any past mistakes and get on with life. Sometimes you just have to lighten the load.

It's a heavy load to carry guilt over past mistakes.

We intentionally keep the load heavy, when we remember all the things we said or did that we wished we hadn't. We go over the scenario again and again, blowing it way out of proportion.

In fact, haven't you ever recalled a moment with someone and found to your surprise that while you have agonized over it and worked it into a matter of great importance, the other person barely remembers the incident? You find you've carried the load, letting it distract you, weigh you down, wasted all this time and energy on it for no reason. It is easy to forget that in the large scale of life, some incidents are very insignificant.

Brenda and Jane were best friends. They liked the same things and enjoyed shopping together. One day in a jewelry shop they were looking at rings. Brenda spied a ring she liked, but since Jane had the salesman's attention, she waited. Jane chose a ring and asked to see it… the same ring that Brenda liked. Jane wanted to buy it but didn't have enough money. Later Brenda decided to go back to the store and see the ring herself. It fit, she loved it, she had the money for it, she bought it. She felt guilty though since it was the same ring that Jane had wanted. For years she avoided wearing it around Jane, but

---

If ignorance is bliss,
why aren't more
people happy?

The mind,
conditioned as it is
by the past, always
seeks to re-create
what it knows and is
familiar with...
- Eckhart Tolle,
The Power of Now

then unexpectedly Jane stopped over one day. Jane noticed the ring and said she remembered it...wasn't that the same ring they had seen years ago in that store? Brenda acknowledged that it was, feeling as guilty as if she had stolen it from her friend. Jane then said she was glad that Brenda went back and bought it. She had decided against it, and besides she never really had the money to buy it anyway. If she couldn't have it, then she was just as happy that Brenda owned it instead. Brenda realized with a shock that all the guilt she had felt over the ownership of the ring had been misplaced for all these years. She had carried a load that existed only in her head, not in reality.

Lighten up!

Make a conscious decision to let go of the past.

When you lighten the load, you make the choice to be done with something and choose to let it go out of your life. You give it permission to slowly slip into the back of your mind, all but disappearing. It is a conscious choice that you make to choose not to remember. How do you do this? As soon as you are aware that you are thinking of something you don't want to think about, stop. Choose another thought, a positive one. You can make another conscious choice: the decision to be happy.

Choose to be positive in the face of negativity.

Whatever happens in any situation, we can choose to remain emotionally detached, unaffected by the situation, outside of the drama. Judges, mediators and negotiators must be able to render unbiased decisions while delving into the most negative of situations. They cannot afford to allow any of this negativity to affect them. It can be done with conscious effort and awareness. It just takes practice.

Situations don't cause stress, our thoughts and subsequent feelings do. If we need proof of this, look how different people react to the same situation. When we are feeling stressed, the trick is to change our thoughts of chaos to thoughts of peace.

How do you do that? Distract yourself with something else. Either find a way to think positive about the situation, or think about something else entirely that is more positive, not stressful. The more you can become emotionally involved in something else, the less

Your pain is the breaking of the shell that encloses your understanding.
- Kahlil Gibran, *The Prophet*

Life must be measured by thought and action, not by time.
- Sir John Lubbock

you will be tied to the issue at hand. Once you can break the emotional bond, you are free to let it go, get over it, and get on with the rest of your life.

Pamela was annoyed with her husband. Although she knew that he generally was inconsiderate when he spoke to her, it still got to her. His words still hurt. Knowing he probably was unaware of how badly his words stung didn't help much. She stewed about it all morning and just couldn't let it go. He was really insufferable and she had to talk to someone, hear a kind voice. On the way to work she called her friend, Kate, looking for an opportunity to vent her aggravation. When Kate answered the phone, Pam found out in the first few minutes that she wasn't having an easy time either. Kate was in the throes of breaking up with her boyfriend. By the time she hung up the phone, Pam found that the aggravation over her own issues was gone. She had become so involved in Kate's problems, she had forgotten about her own. While she was still annoyed at what happened, her emotions had become disentangled from it. She had become emotionally involved with Kate and that managed to break the bond to her own issues.

Most of us find it easier to overlook the mistakes of others, yet continue to be hard on ourselves. As if there wasn't enough in the present to be responsible for, we often insist on dredging up the past to torment ourselves. We have a tendency to set our standards high, often too high to succeed. Then when we fail to meet our own expectations, we criticize ourselves for failing. Recalling past failures is valuable only for remembering the lessons that we learned. Other than that, time and energy spent on resurrecting yesterday is wasted and pointless.

We make mistakes.
That's a fact of life.

Our actions cause other things to happen and so we face the ultimate Law of Cause and Effect. Whether it is a physical fender bender or an emotional heartbreak, we need to learn whatever the lesson is. In that way, good comes from the situation and increases our ability to accept the necessary changes into our life without denying the facts. Negative experiences can be transcended by working through understanding to acceptance, acknowledging the lesson, and then letting the emotion go.

Most folks are about as happy as they
make up their minds to be.
- Abraham Lincoln

Are you ready to
accept the
responsibility that
goes with realizing the
power you have within?
- Bruce D. Schneider,
*Relax, You're Already
Perfect*

You can be just as happy as you make up your mind to be.

It isn't easy, but by consciously changing our thinking about ourselves and others, and learning to live in the present moment, our lives can take a more positive path. The quality of life is all about consciousness. When we make a decision to move beyond thoughts of lack, limitation, and other negative ideas, we make room for new, vigorous, and life-affirming thoughts. If you believe you can do something, a door will open.

Whatever life is showing us, we are responsible for. We put out a cause and we get to experience the effect. If we don't like an experience, before we can change it, we have to take responsibility for it. If we move into victimhood or blame, we misdiagnose the cause and it will never change. Choices can liberate or imprison us. No matter what is going on in our lives, we created it, and therefore we can change it. The choice is ours and so is the responsibility.

People often say that motivation doesn't last.
Well, neither does bathing
that's why we recommend it daily.
- Zig Ziglar

Yesterday ended last night.
- Raymond Charles Barker

First say to yourself what you would be;
and then do what you have to do.
- Epictetus

Chapter 13

The High Road

How You Get It Back

Each morning you wake up is a new day, as yet untouched by anything, totally neutral, full of promise and possibilities. What will you do with it? The choice is yours. It's a choice you make every day, conscious of it or not. Will you take the high road?

Happiness and success are choices.

There is a big difference between wishing it were so,

and choosing to make it so.

You can narrow the chasm between what you enjoy doing and what you are spending your time doing by following a Buddhist suggestion: *Look in the direction you want to go in, and start walking.* Declare each day good from the start, full of promise, and no matter what happens you will reap its benefits. Even when it does not appear that all things are working together for your good, it is still so.

You could have made other choices in your life, but you would not be the same person you are today. To be who you are now requires each step and choice you made from the past. Be thankful for the lessons learned and armed with that knowledge, turn

155

Renew thyself completely each day;
do it again, and again,
and forever again.
- Chinese inscription

Instead of thinking of the problem,
think of the answer.
- Ernest Holmes, *This Thing Called You*

towards the future wide open with possibilities. Each experience you have had, whether it was good or bad, was important. Skipping any of them, you wouldn't be you.

"Every day is a good day."
- a Zen master

This affirmation removes the conditional joy from our lives. When we are not feeling particularly happy, we usually say we'd feel much better if we could only have *this* or *that*. With that item in our lives, then we'd be happy. But that happiness is conditional. It doesn't last long and soon we are off in search of the next thing that will surely make us happy for a very long time.

Focus on Solutions, not Problems.

If you are unhappy with your life, you feel limited, stuck in your problem, and yet the opposite is true. It is instead an opportunity to release your energy into finding new solutions. It's a matter of focusing on the solution rather than the problem, a better choice by far since whatever you give attention to flourishes. It is how you turn negatives that are problems into positive choices that are solutions.

The best choice to be successful
is to start your day in a positive light.

In the morning take a moment to stand in front of the mirror by yourself and affirm that your day will be good. Feel positive energy, generate an energy field, let it surround you. Then face the day knowing only good is coming into your life. Even if some things may appear to be not so good or even awful, if you'll look for the lesson instead of the problem, you'll be able to turn what looks like a negative event into a positive one. The more you do it, the easier it will be, the better you will feel.

Lessons are wake-up calls to pay attention.

Sometimes the universe sends out a cosmic 2x4 to hit you over the head and get your attention. That happens when you are missing some important element and need to be

157

We make a living by what we get.
We make a life by what we give.
- Martin Luther King, Jr.

There are two things
to aim at in life;
first, to get what you want;
after that, to enjoy it.
Only the wisest of mankind
achieve the second.
- Logan Pearsall Smith,
Afterthoughts

reminded. It's a wake up call that will continue to hit until you notice it. Often they get bigger, so it's better to pay attention as soon as you can. *Get* the lesson and then let the emotion go. By doing this, you will maintain a positive attitude no matter what is happening. This is not making a bad thing good, but it does remove the sting.

Sometimes when we are trying to do something, no matter what we do, it just doesn't work. It feels like something is trying to stop us. We put so much emphasis on the fact that we are not getting to where we want to go, that we miss the most important fact. The Lesson. There's a lesson here to be learned. If we don't get the Lesson, then it will just keep on repeating itself until we do or we just give up trying. Giving up doesn't solve anything. It just delays the Lesson until the next opportune moment when it will crop up unannounced and undesired for us to deal with again. We miss the Lesson in our efforts to get to our goal. There are times when the goal is actually of little importance. It may seem extremely important at the time, but in the bigger picture – not so much. That's when the goal exists only for the Lesson we are supposed to be learning. When things are difficult, be aware. Get the Lesson.

You may think you have no choice.

Let's say Friday you had a fight with your boss and almost quit your job, then you got a speeding ticket on the way home. Now it's Monday morning, you wake up. It feels like it's going to be a good day. Then you remember Friday's events and suddenly dread going to work. Your good feelings evaporate from your mind and body to be replaced by worry and anxiety instead. Will you continue to create wave after wave of negative energy? Or, do you direct your thoughts instead to the positive things in your life? Sometimes you may have to search for them. They may even be small. But they are not insignificant.

Dwell and build on the positive or the negative, your choice. Stewing will bring depression as negativity begets more negativity. Bringing positive thoughts to mind will bring back the good feelings you started out with instead.

The choice is yours, every day.

I believe that imagination
is more important than knowledge.
- Albert Einstein,
The World As I See It

Whatever the mind can conceive,
it can achieve.
- Dr. Frederick Bailes

You can't control all situations, but you can control your reaction and determine how much impact an event will have on your day and your life. Will you start with one good thought and spiral up, or remember one negative thing and slide on down?

One thought always leads to another.
Going Up or Down?

When we think about something year after year we tend to perpetuate a condition. What begins in the consciousness seeps down into the subconscious and sets up residence. Change is difficult. How long does it take for the majority of us to break a resolution? For most of us, not long. It is much easier to stay with our comfortable patterns. Change can be incremental, however. We must remember to be kind to ourselves and allow for baby steps that are headed in the right direction.

Whatever purpose you think your life might have, you probably have one thing in common with everyone else: most people would like to make a difference in the world. Making a difference doesn't have to be at the level of Martin Luther King or Mother Theresa, or any other Nobel Peace Prize winner. Making a difference can be as simple as handling a problem for someone, or giving good advice. Some of us can get stuck in just the wondering of how to make a difference when we are already *sooo* busy. All of our time and energy seems to be taken up with just getting by. Yet, the simple truth is if you are alive, you are making a difference. It is up to *you* to decide *how* with what you have to give.

Our task is not to be someone different from who we are, but to bring out what talents are already in us. Our specific gifts were given to us for a purpose. It is our job to make use of them. Using our talents to bring about changes that will make a difference in this world is a lifelong task. Making a difference is not a technique. It is part of the natural activity of being aware and generous with ourselves in whatever areas our talents happen to lie. Many of us live day to day without giving much thought to how we impact our world, and how we daily contribute to it. To stimulate a sense of purpose, all we need to do is focus on what gifts and talents we have and follow through by using them to the best of our ability. What we focus on will increase and manifest more in our lives.

When we take the high road of good cheer,
we are actually extending an invitation to others
to respond in the same good natured way.

...every year will be the result of what we make it,
the result of something that we put into operation
this minute.
- Joel Goldsmith, *Living Now*

"No man is an island."

Ernest Hemingway acknowledged this fact when he penned that famous quote. We are all connected more than we are willing to acknowledge. We affect each other in more ways than we know. This underlying feeling of connection that binds us all together also leaves us wanting at least one other person in our lives. Often we seem to have trouble attracting the right person. We cannot manufacture a friendship by manipulating our behavior to attract someone. It just won't work.

The expression of our thoughts and feelings by word and action must be true with no expectations of return. If we expect a return for anything we offer, then it is out of neediness that we are making the offering. We cannot control how another will respond to us. When we give, we need to do so just for the joy of the giving. If the action is reciprocated then all the better.

Every moment gives you the opportunity to choose the high road.

Choosing the High Road is acting from a higher level of consciousness and awareness, living a conscious way of life. It means choosing to be kind rather than petty in any situation; generous rather than stingy; thinking of someone else first, rather than yourself. Choosing the high road daily takes strength, diligence, and discipline.

It takes discipline to release righteous indignation and to refrain from self condemnation when you are wrong. It takes diligence to avoid negative habit patterns and live a positive life style on purpose. It means standing firm in the strength of your convictions, knowing you know what you know, and not succumbing to the confusion around you.

The past can be seductive, longing for what has been.
It can keep us from moving forward in the present.

We all know the story of Lot in the Bible. Lot's wife couldn't resist turning around, and her thoughts crystallized her like a pillar of salt, leaving her stuck in the past unable to move forward. Similarly, we can crystallize our life by remaining focused on the way

> It is one of the most
> beautiful compensations of
> this life that no man can
> sincerely try to help another
> without helping himself.
> - Ralph Waldo Emerson

> Really to live means to contribute;
> to live means to add something to the
> sum total of the good in the world.
> - Joel Goldsmith,
> *The Attitude of Prayer*

things used to be. This is a waste of time. We can never go back, even when we think we really want to. We must remain open to new ways of thinking for growth to occur.

None of us are here by accident. We all have something to give that only we can offer. If we do not share it, the world is deprived of it forever. As children we took risks all the time. As adults we often fear to go beyond our comfort zones into uncharted territory. The art of success is to know what you want, and be willing to go for it. That means not allowing obstacles or fear to get in the way of your dreams. Everyone has a gift to bring to the world and we need to be willing to move beyond our comfort zones to manifest it. An orchestra needs the sound of each instrument to create the entire musical score. Without any one instrument, the music would be missing a sound. So too, if all of our gifts aren't given to the world, a piece of the big picture will be missing like a hole in a jigsaw puzzle.

Doing the best we can do is all anyone can ask of us. We know when we do our best, and when we don't. We are in charge of our actions, but not the results of our actions. It has been said that the steps on Buddha's eight-fold path are right *action*, not right *result*. Success means doing all we can to develop our talents as fully as we are able. Sometimes we can fall into the trap of believing that only a select few have talents and certainly we aren't one of *them*. Yet in reality we each have unlimited potential, limited only by our belief systems. If we can dream it, we can be it or do it.

You unlock the door to your talents by believing they are there. Assume the possibility that the talent exists, create a space for it, and then give it permission to manifest. Listen to your Inner Authority. Look to what attracts you. Once you discover it, nourish it by taking some action every day to bring your gift into reality. Each step leads to another, even baby steps.

Just begin.

Whose life are you living, yours or the one somebody prefers for you? If you allow others to unduly influence your choices, you will never be able to deliver your uniqueness to the world. You have the responsibility to live and lead your own life.

The best way to cheer yourself up
is to try to cheer someone else up.
- Mark Twain

It is never about what's actually happening,
it's how we choose to think about what is happening.

No matter what happens, somebody will
find a way to take it too seriously.

Chapter 14

Stop the Ripple Effect

Some people just like to complain. It's what they do. Some people complain more than others. Does that mean that they have more to complain about, that they're just more vocal in general, or is it simply how they view the world and their place in it?

It seems to be a human tendency to complain,
some of us at the slightest provocation.

We all complain on occasion. We can take on the weather, the news, the scenery, the traffic, whatever occupies us at the time. We can complain when things don't go our way, and even when they do. Anything that deviates from our personal preference of how we think things should be, we can take a moment to complain about it. Are things really that bad?

A complaint is simply a negative interpretation of a neutral event.

What we complain about, we are focusing on. What we give our attention to grows. So basically the more we complain and focus our attention on unwanted circumstances, the more we are going to have them in our lives. Without realizing it, we are actually working against ourselves creating more of what we don't want.

The obstacle is the path.
- Zen Saying

Do not anticipate trouble, or worry what
may never happen. Keep in the sunlight.
- Benjamin Franklin

When you find yourself complaining, STOP.

Try to see the situation from a neutral perspective.

If we can learn to complain less, we will automatically have less to complain about. Besides complaining, the other tendency we all seem to have is to worry – about everything and nothing. Why?

Even though all evidence shows that worrying achieves nothing,

our belief seems to be that if we worry about it,

we can stop it from happening.

Which only illustrates how wrong we can be. Focusing on the problem can cause a downward spiral. It means there is no attention given to finding the solution. We cannot fix the problem at the level of the problem. When we cease to concern ourselves with the how and the where, the answer to our dilemma has room to appear.

Taking responsibility for ourselves... what exactly does that mean? Have you ever said, "Now look what you made me do!"

It's easier to blame someone else for your actions,

than accept that only you are responsible for your choices.

To effect a change, all you have to do is *change your own thinking* which luckily you control. You do not have to try to change someone else to get positive results.

If you maintain that someone else did it *to* you, that diminishes the power you have to handle the problem. Since we always choose that which we will benefit from the most, we need to determine what benefit we are receiving from a negative situation. Attention, sympathy, or even a closer relationship are possible benefits. Many people's lives are a repetition of patterns moving from crisis to crisis. As soon as one situation is dealt with, another arises to take its place.

Sometimes we feel so burdened by feelings of hopelessness and despair that we can't see our way to daylight. We have told our stories of woe so many times, we have become

If you tell the truth,
you don't have to remember anything.

Forgive others and forgive yourself.
You have that power.
-W. Frederick Keeler

them. Even though the events happened long ago, we live them over again and generate more suffering each time we tell them. But we are not our stories.

You can even participate in a commiserating club, a pity party, where you can swap your pity stories with others. Only the characters change as you move from person to person. Each recitation, being terrible, affirms how bad things are. The way out is to take responsibility for your choices, acknowledge you just may have something to do with your life being the way it is. When you are in charge of your life, your choices will flow in the direction you want to go.

When we allow others to upset us, make us angry or resentful, we give up control of our lives to them.

Now someone else will determine how we will feel. When we sit in judgment of another, deciding whether the action was right or wrong, not only does it affect us negatively, but it also denies others their right to choose.

Sheila and Craig were moving to another state. He found a job but it started before the house they were buying was ready. So Craig moved with just a few of his belongings and stayed at a friend's house. A few weeks later Sheila was driving down for the closing on their new home. Craig asked her to rent a trailer and bring several boxes and his motorcycle down with her as he had not been able to bring them when he'd left. She reluctantly agreed. Later Sheila realized a simple trip had become very complicated. She had to rent a truck since their van had been in a recent accident. She was now driving with two children, for 12 hours through several states with heavy traffic, in an unfamiliar rented vehicle, pulling a rented trailer that was holding a motorcycle and boxes. Plus she had to find a way to load the trailer. Sheila felt it was too much for her to handle. She wanted to make her husband happy but not at the price she had to pay. The stress level was too high for such a long trip. She called him back and said she would drive down but not with a trailer. It was the best she could do. Craig became angry. He felt she had made a wrong decision. There was no reason that she couldn't do him this favor. Craig had a choice to make. He could continue to judge Sheila, insist that she change her decision, and hang on to his anger. This would upset both of them, and deny Sheila the

Before you criticize someone,
you should walk a mile in their shoes.
That way, when you criticize them
you're a mile away and you have their shoes.

Depression is merely anger
without enthusiasm.

right to choose what she felt was the correct thing to do. Or he could understand that Sheila was under enough stress already because of the move, and let it all go.

If someone fails to measure up to your standards,

that failure exists only in your mind.

In reality there is no failure. Yet since you feel the choice was incorrect, you are forced to experience the failure. Now you're stuck with a negative emotion which you will have to either dismiss or let it upset you causing yet another negative ripple. The alternative is to refrain from judgment or even comparison. Let the action just be neutral, a past event over which you have no control.

Staying on the positive path is not easy.

If you want the easy way out, you can let every annoyance get to you and fill yourself full of negative energy. You can choose to generate that negative energy continuously if you like, until it fills your life. Many people do. Negative energy has a certain charge to it that can feel very powerful. It can give you the false impression that you feel very good, invincible, tough. The illusion disguises the fact that underneath it your self esteem and self respect are gone.

It's easy to criticize, judge, put down anyone and anything. The difficult choice is to look for the positive and stay with it. It's not easy to put on a happy face when you feel anything but. It's hard to let it be when you are outraged. But if you don't let your anger go, the negative energy won't end there. It will continue thought by thought, like stepping stones leading down a path to an inevitable destination. It will spread ripple by ripple and drag you down with it. It's not easy to stay positive, but it is the better, wiser choice. You constantly generate energy. You must choose whether it's negative or positive - will you benefit or suffer? You must remember that you are not the victim here, you always have control over what you think, how you feel.

You can never alter causal events, but each day, moment by moment,

you have a choice whether to continue a thought process or not.

173

Did you ever notice
how difficult it is
to argue with
someone who is not
obsessed with
being right?
- Wayne Dyer

Nonattachment means you flow on top of the water.
You don't plunge into it.
You stay afloat without going under.
- Dipa Ma, Knee Deep in Grace

Your thoughts can lead you up or down. Only you can make that determination. You are the only one who has control over your reactions and subsequent actions. When you decide something is bad, refuse to accept it, and get upset, all you've succeeded in doing is doubling the negative.

Everything is positive until you have your first negative thought formed by a judgment or criticism. That's number one. That's the stone thrown into the pond. The first ripple from the impact of that negative thought in a sea of calm is registering that thought in your body. Your body gets upset and lets you know in some manner. Your body can become rigid, your hands can clench, your arms crossed in front of you. Your feelings suddenly change to unhappy, sad, angry, lonely, depressed. You haven't changed what has happened. All you've done is spread the negativity by allowing it to affect you.

Choose to stop the ripple of negativity.

Since none of us are alone, negativity can spread to others as long as we each choose to keep it going. The Ripple Effect is like what happens when a pebble is dropped in a pond. Visually you can see the ripples spread out from the central point where the pebble fell. In the same manner when an event happens, its effect can be spread over many other events and people. Much like a stink in the air, it slowly spreads outward poisoning everything it envelops.

When an event takes place, it's neutral until you decide it's bad. Once you decide it's bad, you become upset. Then you can take your negative mood out on the next person, and they can take it out on the following person they encounter – and so on, and so on. To stop the ripple effect, all any one person has to do is refuse to not take on the projected, repeated negativity. Should something negative hit you, accept it as an event that happened and let it be. Otherwise all you do is make yourself and everyone around you miserable. Like spreading a disease, it is a dis-ease of the spirit. Stop the ripple effect, don't pass it along.

The actual cause of a particular ripple of negativity could be many, many people and instances away from the present moment, yet it can still be having an effect because each person is willing to pass it along. Often hours and days after an unpleasant incident,

What is hateful to you do not do to your neighbor.
That is the whole Torah. The rest is commentary.
- Hillel, 6th Century, *Talmud*

We are responsible for
every word we express.
It will affect somebody
for good or otherwise.
- Christian Lars,
The Ideal Made Real

we're still rehashing the scene, creating clever retorts we never delivered, telling others about our awful experience, and by doing so we keep generating more negative energy.

Anyone lashing out at you is generally doing so from a position of ignorance or insensitivity.

Some days we tend to feel like everyone is out to get us, but that's not true. When we feel that way, we tend to strike out offensively to ward off further imagined attacks before they have a chance to happen. Basically, an "I'll get you before you get me" attitude puts us on the defense. It is seldom meant as a personal attack even though that's the way it feels when you are the recipient.

It's not about you, even when you feel like it is.

You can feel like a target when someone projects his anger upon you. Anyone who reacts in this manner does so out of habit. You aren't the first and certainly won't be the last person to be treated this way. Once you see the truth of the situation and realize it's not about you at all, you can avoid taking it personally. Then when it is over, it will have no claim on you and you will be able to let it go with ease.

The best reaction is to examine the incident to determine if it is personal in any way. If it needs to be addressed, do so. If not, let it go and be done with it, because it wasn't about you in the first place. No one has the right to be unkind to you. There is no reason to ever torment yourself about it.

Don't *take* it personally.
Don't *make* it personal.

> *Know Thyself.*
> *Inscription at the Delphic Oracle*
> *- Plutarch, Morals*

Some days you are the bug;
some days you are the windshield.

One must have the adventurous daring
to accept oneself as a bundle of possibilities
and undertake the most interesting game in the world,
making the most of one's best.
- Harry Emerson Fosdick

Chapter 15

Things We Do

A Wrap Up

We all begin life with self esteem. As a baby gains awareness, he thinks he is okay. He has no reason to think otherwise. Self Esteem is simply a person's realistic respect for himself. Essential for success is good self esteem or having a favorable impression of oneself. Depending how life treats you and what you do about it, some of us have more and lose less self esteem then others. Some of us have it easier and some of us have traveled a more rocky road. Experience life but when life gets difficult, and it will, guard your self esteem. Avoid those people who, although they mean well, will only bring you down, and cultivate time with those who choose to support you.

We all live with expectations. Parents have expectations for their children. Each new job and new relationship comes with its own set of expectations. Expectations are important. If we expect nothing, we get nothing. When expectations are low, there is no reason to struggle and achieve more. When they are unrealistically high, defeat waits off stage in the wings. Living a conscious way of life means being honest and realistic with yourself, while honoring the gift of believing in yourself and what you are capable of.

179

Guilt is not meeting the expectations of
others, imagined or real.
- Jennifer James, *Visions from the Heart*

Everything and everybody is going to change,
so why fight it?
Why not be one of those who says,
let's see what I can change to improve things?
- Robert Anthony, *Total Self Confidence*

We can fail to meet someone's expectations, or they can fail to meet ours. The offending party is usually subject to an unending stream of criticism laced heavily with disappointment. Although motivated by the best of intentions, rather than producing the desired results of improvement, the reaction is most often the opposite. The failing party becomes unresponsive, rebellious, falling into a downward spiral that is hard to reverse. This provokes low self esteem so the person doesn't care about himself, or anyone or anything else. That's when family and friends are abused. Animals are abused. The environment suffers. It all just goes downhill with the negativity feeding on itself until and unless that person decides to change.

Stress is a part of life. There is really no way to be free of it, especially because it comes in so many forms. The best way to handle stress is by finding another way to look at the situation. A positive viewpoint will reduce stress.

If you see something that is unjust and it can be changed, then take action to change it. Put to good use the energy you generate when you are upset, rather than wallow in it feeling bad, getting angry. If nothing can be done about it, like taking issue with the weather, then do what you can and let it go. Focus on the positives that the experience generates instead of the negatives. Most things have at least two sides. It is your choice which you will focus on to generate more of the same type thoughts and corresponding energy.

When you become emotionally involved in a negative occurrence, you feel bad. Now that feeling bad can last just a moment or two, or you can hang on to it and build it into a real pity-pot. You can feel as sorry for yourself as you have a mind to. Sit in that pity-pot as long as you want. Wallow in all the "poor me" that you can dredge up. Stay there until you're done feeling sorry for yourself. Then get up, get over it, and get on with the rest of your life. There's lots more to come and you're bound to feel this way many more times. Life ain't for sissies.

We often make decisions based on incorrect information. As much as we don't want to be, we seem to be a species that specializes in passing judgment. We tend to judge everything and everyone that we encounter without much thought as to whether we are right or wrong.

Never put both
feet in your mouth
at the same time,
because then
you don't have a leg
to stand on.

Stand up for yourself,
but not by pushing anyone else around.

For example, we could see a vehicle driving towards us covered in mud. We might wonder why it is so dirty and assume that the driver doesn't take care of his vehicle. But let's say that as it comes closer and we can see more than just the front of it, we see that the dirt is sprayed along the side. As it passes us, we are able to see that the back is actually clean. That tells us that the vehicle was clean and the mud spray probably came from someone else driving through a puddle and splashing the front as it passed. Thinking that the driver didn't care about keeping a clean vehicle would have been an erroneous assumption because of incomplete information. We tend to think we know enough about a situation to form a decision quickly, yet often this is not the case. That's when we say, "But I thought that..." and the reality is we are wrong.

We all do it. Criticize. And to what end when we all are aware that no one responds well to a constant barrage of criticism and negativity. Why doesn't it work? Because once again we are trying to change the wrong person...someone else, not us. If criticizing *more* doesn't get the right results, perhaps criticizing *less* will. Criticizing what is missing places the emphasis on what is wrong. Expressing praise, gratitude and appreciation places emphasis on what has been done well instead. This provokes a response to do better, try harder – the exact result we were hoping for when we started all the criticism in the first place.

Most people have control issues. Simply, we want things to go our way. We want to be in control. We are happiest then. Those of us who do wake up, becoming aware of exactly what is going on, i.e., we want things done our way, the right way, also realize that we can't have it our way all of the time. This is actually good however, because although struggle is hard and inconvenient, it is the way we learn. Generally, what we first start learning is the other guy's position. Once we find we are at odds instead of in agreement, we have a choice of forcing our way or compromising. Interestingly enough, we gain the power to influence others only when we stop trying to control them. Acquiescing to another's wishes, generally makes them grateful and can put you in control.

In the area of relationships when things are not quite what we had in mind, we expect the other person to bridge the gap, not us. Relationships have a predestined end when we expect to change the behavior of anyone other than ourselves. Basically, when we say

The first step toward not being
unconsciously influenced by something
was to become conscious of it.
- Dass, *Still Here*

No pessimist
ever discovered
the secret of the stars,
or sailed to an uncharted land,
or opened a new doorway for
the human spirit.
- Helen Keller

someone makes us angry, we have ceded power and control over to them. We are also saying that it is their behavior that must change in order for our anger to cease. Since we cannot control their behavior as much as we would like to, the more we try to control them and fail, the angrier we become. Once we recognize the futility of this and realize how foolish it is to allow someone else to make us angry, we can choose not to go there. We gain back our control.

When you say, "You make me angry" it really is not so. What you have said is that you have no control over your emotions. You have given your power away to someone else so they have power over you instead. Think about it. In effect you are saying, "Here, take control of me. Control how I will feel, how my day will be." Why would you want to do this? Why would you want to give someone else that kind of power over you? Wouldn't you rather retain your power so that *you* determine how you want to feel? *You* decide what kind of day you will have.

All of us have people in our lives who are negative. We wish they were more positive for we believe that they and we would be happier. Basically, we want them to change. The truth is that free advice and fancy ideas won't change people until they are ready to change. Trying to change them will only irritate them. In our attempts to make them more positive we end up creating more negativity.

It's all about attitude. Change your attitude if you can't change the circumstances. You will find that positive thinking will bring about positive results. Enjoy any moments when you feel really good. It could be as simple a thing as a beautiful day driving home from work for the weekend, listening to your favorite music. Really appreciating the small moments generates more energy in that direction to attract and produce more of the same.

When you rise in the morning, you can choose to shine all day no matter what happens. If anything does not go your way, make a decision to let go of control over it – especially if you have no choice and do not have the power to change it to your liking. Your power extends only over the way you feel and act, nothing else. So use your power over what you can control, *you*. Stay positive. Refuse to get sucked into a downward negative spiral. Look for the good. It's often hiding, but examine the issue from all sides.

Throw off yesterday as a snake sheds its skin.
- Joseph Campbell

The great thing about life is
that as long as we live
we have the privilege of growing.
- Joshua Loth Liebman

Like a many faceted crystal, turn it around until one of those angles shows you something good or at least a lesson learned. Get it. Understand it. Grok it. Then let the negative emotion attached to it go as soon as you are able. Distance yourself from it. Zone in on something good in your life to occupy your mind until you regain your balance. Use your Gratitude Rock to turn the tide of negative energy. Redirect your thoughts to the positive and your energy will follow.

If you drive a car, there's a pretty decent chance that at some point during your driving career you will have the unfortunate experience of hitting an animal on the road. It happens – be it a bird, snake, squirrel, rabbit, cat or dog. Some people feel no remorse while others can't dismiss the accident so quickly and are overwrought with guilt or grief. This is an instance that is difficult to find any good in. Since you can't undo the accident, all you can do is to think differently about it. It was that animal's destiny to be killed at that moment of time. You simply happened by and had to play your part in the brief drama. It really wasn't about you at all. It was about the fulfillment of another's destiny. It did not matter if it was you or someone else. It just happened to be you. So get over it.

Try this technique to separate yourself emotionally from an incident: See yourself standing by a swiftly flowing river. At your feet is a box. Make it small or large, any style, your choice. Place your problem in the box, close it up, and then tie a rope around it. Grab the other end of the rope and throw the box into the current. You see the rope trailing out on the water until it pulls taut. You can hold onto that box as long as you want to keep your problem. When you are ready to let go of your problem, let go of the rope. As you watch the box float away from you, getting smaller in the distance until you can't see it any more, let the emotion of the issue float away with it. Just let it drift away from your mind until you can't feel it any more.

If you want to judge how your life is going, you don't do it by comparing yourself to others. You can't really tell much about your life by looking at the lives of those around you. On the outside anyone can appear to be happy, but on the unknown inside anything can be going on. So comparing yourself to others is delusion. The only meaningful comparison anyone can make is that of comparing your own life today to any yesterday. Life changes constantly. You are not the same person you were last year. Experiences have changed you in both discreet and obvious ways for living requires constant growth.

Whatever you may think of the question
of free will, the truth is your
experiences throughout your life are
determined by your assumptions —
whether conscious or unconscious.
- Neville, *The Power of Awareness*

Learn to think about what you wish to become.
- Ernest Holmes, *This Thing Called Life*

You have been either happy or sad, both being transient feelings. Real happiness is growing and changing, developing your life to the fullest. Trying to be someone else, or what you think someone wants you to be will result in dismal failure. Discover your talents. Use your gifts wisely. Be who you are and do it well.

Choose to maintain your integrity - being true to who you are, who you were meant to be. It can be said that a cardboard box has integrity when it maintains the rigid shape it was constructed for. Once it is damaged, it loses its integrity and falls apart. So too, you will not be you unless you remain true to yourself. That is where your strength lies, in your integrity. Lose it, and you will also fall apart.

> You are a child of the universe,
> no less than the trees and the stars;
> you have a right to be here.
> And whether or not it is clear to you,
> no doubt the universe is unfolding as it should.
> - Max Ehrman

> How do you find your way back in the dark?
> Just head for that big star straight on.
> - Arthur Miller, *The Misfits*

> Each of us has within our grasp
> an Aladdin's lamp of limitless power.
> - Emery John Michael, *Jewels of Light*

Chapter 16

Show Me the Way

to go Home

We come into this life as babies. If we appeared in this form on an alien planet, the beings there would question us. *Who are you? Why are you here? What is your purpose?* If we were able to answer, our reply would be that basically we have no freaking idea. As it is though, when we appear on planet Earth someone automatically takes care of us without asking those questions.

We don't enter this world with the innate knowledge of knowing what to do and why. It's more like coming in with amnesia. Most of us usually spend our lives wandering around a great deal trying to answer these questions. As we grow, we realize that the answers are important to us. We have no map, no plan, no known destination. No idea of where we are going, or why, until the answers start coming our way. Many of us get lost in the smoke and mirrors and flashing lights which only confuse us more. We are constantly buffeted by experiences, some uplifting and others crushing. Some push us in the flow. Some blow us off course. Some of us are so asleep we don't even know that we are lost. Unless we remember to stay aware, we can lose our way over and over again. Each time it happens we have to renew our search, once more attempting to figure out just how to find our way home.

191

Each of us, as we
journey through
life, has the
opportunity to find
and to give his or
her unique gift.
- Helen Luke

Bring such talents as you have, use them,
and they will be multiplied.
- Ernest Holmes, *Words That Heal Today*

"Show me the way to go home," is an old song as well as a mantra of mine. It means let me fulfill the purpose of my life, the reason I am here. Once I figure that out and do it, I am free to go home again. Each of us has our own special talents, gifts we have been given to use. Although many people live like they believe the axiom "He who dies with the most toys, wins," I don't believe that is the truth. I don't believe that the purpose of life is to simply collect toys, i.e., accumulate possessions and party on down.

I believe that we are here to fulfill our life's purpose. How do you discover your life's purpose? Look to your talents. Think of what you like to do. The reason you like to do it is because it comes easy for you. What comes easy for you to do are your talents. We all have different ones to offer. They were given to us for a purpose – to use them to the best of our ability doing as much good as we can, and as little harm as possible.

All of our individual talents are like various sized buckets filled with different colors. Each color is a talent. Our job is to use all of the color in the bucket, whether it's a quart or five gallon size. If all you have is only a cup, then that is what you have to give. Be sure to use all of it.

One of my talents is that I get along well with animals. Animals like me and know I like them and wish them no harm. But I'm not a singer, nor an actress, nor a surgeon. I'm not a dentist, nor can I carve ice sculptures with a chain saw. They're not my talents. I am good with my hands. I can also write, teach, counsel, and cook. I enjoy doing all of these things for they come easily to me. I have learned to play a few musical instruments. I can do it but it doesn't flow naturally. I have to work at it, so I can tell you that music is not where my talents lie.

You may like working with people, or you may not. You may like working with your hands at any craft, or you may find you have no dexterity with tools. You may like to cook and be good at it, or you may be better off pushing the button on the microwave. Plants may respond well to your care, or they may wilt instead of thrive. All of your talents and gifts put together form the pattern for your life purpose. Follow your heart and it will show you the way to go home.

Each of us has a part in the orchestra of life. We each have our own instrument to play, our own particular notes. If we don't play our part, then a piece of the music isn't

The world is your exercise book -
the pages upon which you do your sums.
- Richard Bach, *Illusions*

*Pleasure in the job
puts perfection in the work.
- Aristotle*

there. The tune would have silence where your notes should be, much like a pattern of threads missing in a tapestry. What comes naturally for you is your particular gift. Play it and play it well.

Whatever you do, do your best. Whether it's slicing meats in a deli, answering phones or washing dishes, just do your best. If you're assigned a task you don't care for, still do it to the best of your ability. If you don't like what you are doing, then change it if you can. But sometimes we can't. Sometimes we must do things we don't particularly care to do. When that happens, honor yourself and the work you are doing by still doing it to the best of your ability with diligence, kindness, gratitude, and respect. Act with responsibility for your actions and choices.

You'll make mistakes. That's okay. Actually that's not only okay, it's part of the plan. It's a learning process. That's the way life works here. The important part is to get the lesson. Learn what the experience is trying to teach you. Because if you don't get it the first time, no matter how much it may have cost you, you will repeat the same experience again and again until you do learn the lesson. That is why similar experiences continue to occur in your life, as in the "why do these things always happen to me?" syndrome. They will continue to repeat until you wake up. When you miss the cue of the more subtle nudges, the lesson can hit you like a 2x4 to get your attention. I can tell you that hurts, so try and get it as soon as possible.

Some of us are givers and some of us are takers who fail to reciprocate in kind. A problem givers often have is that they get so engrossed in giving, they forget the reciprocal of receiving. In the act of taking care of yourself, you become the giver and the receiver. Allowing you to give to yourself and receiving from others are big lessons. If you don't pay attention, the lesson can become a disability. The longer you take to get it, the bigger the lesson will get; so it is extremely important to learn to pay attention. Everyone has things happen and the same things happen to many of us. It is not *what* happens, but how we handle it – what we do with the experience – that counts.

The trick about planet Earth is its physicality. This is what makes it so beautiful and so difficult. We have a lot of attractions on many levels. The trick is to not get lost in the smoke and mirrors, not get all wrapped up in it and lose our way. At any moment over

*Everything we say and do
has an effect on the fabric of humanity.
- Gandhi*

Every crucial experience can be regarded as a setback
- or the start of a new kind of development.
- Mary Roberts Rinehart

any item, we run the danger of getting sucked into the distraction, "Whoever dies with the most toys, wins" and forget what life is all about.

When anything happens, we have no way of knowing the kind of impact, good or bad, our actions will have on ourselves, others or the environment. We have no way of seeing the really big picture. When things go wrong (we're late for an appointment, we fail to receive something we want or lose something precious) we have no way of knowing what type of impact it will have on our lives. 9/11 is an excellent example. How many stories have we heard of people who were supposed to be there, but were held up by unforeseen events. Many things happen to us during our lives which are less catastrophic but still of major importance.

Charlie was negotiating for a house and was just about to sign the papers, when the owner died. The heirs took possession, decided to overvalue it and increased the price. Charlie could no longer afford it. Then an inspection showed the house was full of radon. The loss of having the deal fall through then became a gain. Later it became even more of a gain, when he found a better, nicer house for less money.

When you can't fix the situation, then the best you can do is to get over it. Let any negative feelings of loss flow on out of your mind. Distract yourself with something else to fill the void. Know that the next time, you will find something better. There is always a reason, a lesson. It may have been a protective measure that you needed. This applies to all situations, any kind of missed opportunity. Some of those misses become fortunate outcomes down the road.

The impact that any one of us can have is what scientists have referred to as the Butterfly Effect. Physicists have a theory that the flap of a butterfly's wings in Brazil can set off a storm in Texas. The theory explains how the breeze produced by a butterfly's wings could set off a series of reverberations that over time have a tremendous affect on weather patterns thousands of miles away. The reverberations from our actions can often have a tremendous effect on the world beyond which any of us can see.

Horses that used to roam free on Easter Island had to be corralled to prevent them from eating a poisonous plant growing on the island. At an earlier time, someone had imported the plant from Russia to prevent soil erosion. While curing one problem, they

As you forget self in service to others,
you will find that, without seeking it,
your own cup of happiness will be full.
- Paramahansa Yogananda,
Where There Is Light

If the only prayer you said in your whole life was,
"thank you," that would suffice.
- Meister Eckhart

unknowingly caused a consequence that was much worse. The plant had spread like wildfire. During the fall and winter months it was the most easily available food source for the animals. Now the bigger problem was how to eliminate the plant. An act that was done presumably with good intent had produced dire unforeseen consequences.

While we can seldom know the long reaching effects of our actions, we are bound to do all things with an attitude of Diligence, Kindness, Gratitude, and Respect. Choosing to live a conscious way of life means living every day of our lives keeping this in mind.

In law we are told to practice "due diligence" in our affairs which means to exercise the degree of care and caution required by the circumstances. Practicing Diligence in life is to apply constant and earnest effort to accomplish what is undertaken. In other words, what ever you do, do it well, to the best of your ability. It is of no importance whether or not what you are doing is to your liking.

Act with Kindness. Be kind both to yourself and all other life forms on this planet. Treat all things well including animals and the environment. A little kindness can go a long way. It can save the life of a person, an animal and our planet before it's too late. Even a small act can have tremendous consequences that are unknown to you.

Do all things with Gratitude in your heart. Be grateful for all that you can do and the fact you are capable of doing it. Give thanks for everything in your life, as well as life itself. Life and the opportunity to constantly learn is a gift we receive every morning, even when it feels like a burden.

Respect yourself and others. Pay attention to personal boundaries and objections. With respect comes responsibility, so be responsible for your thoughts, words, and actions. Honor the other life forms that inhabit this planet. Each has its place and purpose. Respect that.

This population of planet Earth by humanity is a study of contrasts, some contrasts having dire consequences for other members of the human race and the environment. Our fellow inhabitants, our furry and non-furry animal friends, as well as the planet itself are not being cared for properly. They deserve respect. Some of us give the respect that is due others, and some of us don't.

And when you get the choice to sit it out or dance,
I hope you dance.
- Mark Sanders and Tia Sillers,
I Hope You Dance

Nothing happens next. This is it.
- Gahan Wilson

When we don't, each of us suffers the consequences. People abuse each other, animals, and Mother Earth, and somehow manage to believe that everything is A-OK. Well it isn't because we're killing Mother Earth and endangering her inhabitants.

We were all put on this planet Earth for a purpose, and we won't be leaving until we get that purpose done. How do we find our purpose? Check our talents and abilities. We each have been given particular abilities that fit our life purpose. It is up to us to figure out what those talents are and then use them to the best of our ability.

Whether you believe in the Eastern view of God where we are all one because God is all there is, nothing is separate or not-God, or believe in the Western view where God is a separate entity who when prayed to will deliver us, either way we are all connected. We are all energy. What affects one, through the ripple effect, eventually affects us all. Like the butterfly effect, it spreads.

Change your thinking and your life will follow. Your thoughts control your life. It's your choice every day to either choose the bad, which is quite often easier and sometimes more popular, or the good. Have high self esteem, think well of yourself, treat yourself and others with respect. Take responsibility for yourself and all you produce through your words, thoughts and actions.

Diligence - Kindness - Gratitude - Respect

Do it Well. Do it Kindly. Do it with Thanks. Do it with Honor.

No matter what happens,
no matter how much your life changes,
one thing is certain,
it is always now.
- Eckhart Tolle

Being in the present is the miracle
by which we master and restore ourselves.
- Thich Nhat Hanh

The best time to plant a tree is twenty
years ago. The next best time is today.
- Ancient Proverb

Chapter 17

Back to the Future

$\mathcal{T}$he Key to the Universe, The Key to the Secret, to having everything you want, to happiness, to success is your attitude. Your attitude will either get you everything or it will get you nothing. It's up to you.

You project your attitude in your tone of voice. Your tone says everything. The words you say matter a great deal, but of utmost importance is *how* you say it. Is it sincere or sarcastic? Complimentary or derogatory? The tone of your body language adds emphasis. Arms open or closed? Are you receptive or defensive?

You can lay all the groundwork humanly possible in the physical to accomplish something, but if your attitude is negative, it won't happen. You'll be your own worst enemy as your negativity undermines your best efforts. If you do not believe in the outcome or if you cannot imagine yourself in that outcome, it will not come to pass. When you desire some thing and it doesn't manifest, the reason is that you're missing the magical combination of the ingredients, thought and feeling, that you must have. Either you did not have a definite image, a clear enough picture of the thing desired to be able to construct a mental equivalent, or your desire wavered destroying any true feeling of it, dissipating any energy. The most powerful moment of creation is in consciousness. Before you can create

You do not exist to impress the world.
You exist to live your life
in a way that will make you happy.
- Richard Bach

Manifestation is not magic. It is the process
of working with natural principles and laws in
order to translate energy from one level of
reality to another.
- David Spangler

a thing or condition, you must be able to imagine yourself having it, and further, be able to *feel* yourself having it.

Often the reason you cannot imagine or feel your desire is because you have endless mind chatter going on, generating resistance to the very thing you say you want. You start with a thought, add the feeling, then distract yourself with fear and worry. Or you might mention to a friend how excited you are about your new prospects, but instead of support, all you hear are the reasons why it won't work. This redirects your feelings away from what you say you want. Well-meant intentions can result instead in your defeat. Remember that you are the only one who can move your feelings around. You can blame others for their negative comments and attitudes, but it is you who causes the change and stems the flow. The Universe is constantly giving. So if you are not getting what you want, you're the problem, not the Universe. You can know with certainty that if you are not resisting somehow, you would have the very thing you say you desire. If you want it, you must feel like you already have it.

Remember that the Universe is your catalog. Figure out what it is that you want. Exactly what it is. Not how you will get it. Just precisely, as precise as you can be, what it is. Place your order. Expect in no uncertain terms to have it delivered. Make a space in your consciousness and your life for it. Do you realize what this then creates? A vacuum. And Space, Time, and Universal Law hate a vacuum. A void must be filled.

It's as if Universal Law looks at you and sees you holding an empty box. You can't have an empty box. It's against the Law. The box must be filled. So Universal Law looks inside and finds your order form all filled out with exactly what you are expecting. A gift list. Well, the Law is the Law so your order must be filled. Universal Law is bound to fill the box with exactly what you asked for. You just have to Ask.

Ask for exactly what you want. Expect to receive it. Act "as if " you already have it. Feel the experience of actually possessing it, all that excitement. Allow those good feelings to fill your consciousness. After all, you are expecting a big package to arrive any day now. You ordered it. It's coming. Generate all the excitement of having it. Working from where you are now to where you want to be can be quite a jump. It may even seem impossible. So just how do you create enthusiasm for having something you don't have yet?

You cannot prevent the birds of sorrow
from flying around your head,
But you can prevent them
from making nests in your hair.
- Chinese Proverb

Your life is the product of your awareness.
Every choice follows from that, and so does every step of growth.
- Deepak Chopra

Turn back time and recall something you received that you really, really wanted. How it meant the world to you. Your heart beat a little faster. Your eyes were brighter. You felt all tingly inside, like your nerves were bursting with energy. You felt alive. Excited. All bright and bushy-tailed. This is how you will feel when it happens, when it is finally yours. Feel that way now as often as you can. The energy you thus generate will send out a magnetic wave attracting it to you.

That doesn't mean, however, that you sit back and wait for it, doing nothing to bring it into manifestation. You need to work with whatever you have to make your dream a reality. Prepare for it, whatever it takes. Do whatever it is that you must do to be ready. If you were giving a party, you wouldn't just announce it and expect it to happen. You have to prepare a space: choose a room, clean and decorate it, arrange the seating, decide on a menu, etc. If you want a career, you need the necessary investment of your time and energy, research and education that will enable it to come to pass. Sitting on a park bench and wishing you had the career, isn't going to give it to you. Universal Law doesn't hit you with a magic wand and "poof!" there you have it.

Take responsibility for your experiences both good and bad. Life sends us the same lesson until we learn it. The fact is, we get what we put our attention on whether we want it or not. So if we concentrate on our problems we get more of them. When we put our minds on what we want, we manifest our dreams. So focus on what you want in your life, rather than on the fact that you don't have it, why you don't have it, or why someone else has it. What you put your attention on is what you will manifest, so it is crucial to put your attention on what is important rather than what may seem pressing at the moment. First, take the time to find out what matters most, then set it as your priority. Keep it in the front of your mind. Intentions are powerful.

The closer your vision is to your heart's desires, the easier it will be to see yourself in it and to believe in what you see. No matter what your particular life's purpose may be, part of it is to live a life that is full of inspiration, joy and passion. You are not here to just drag yourself through your allotted time, knowing at day's end there is yet another unfulfilling day happening tomorrow. The universe supports you one hundred percent when you follow your dream and give the gift you came to give.

The greatest danger for most of us
lies not in setting our aim too high,
But in setting our aim too low and achieving our mark.
- Michelangelo

Do not build up obstacles in your imagination.
- Norman Vincent Peale

One of the greatest gifts we have been given is the ability to choose what our life will be, to choose our experiences. If we can dream it, we can do it. But often fear holds us in place and we procrastinate. For most of us there are times when we are afraid. Fear can limit us, shut us down, make us avoid challenges which cause us to miss opportunities to grow. If we want more out of life, we have to be willing to rid ourselves of thoughts and feelings that act as obstacles to how we want to live, and move beyond what we are comfortable with.

The difficulty for most of us in this physical experience is resisting the impulse to limit ourselves by setting our own boundaries beyond which we think we cannot go. We do this by the words we speak about ourselves, our expectations of the possibilities for our lives and the limited way in which we see ourselves. Actually there are no limits – only those we establish for ourselves. We are free to achieve all of our potential or we can choose to not grow at all. We were given the ability to dream because we were also given the ability to make our dreams come true.

A funny story: while I was working with this material, I suddenly felt as if I were standing in front of a glass door, seeing my reflection in it. On the other side was where I wanted to be. I was right there, that close to having everything I had worked for and wanted. I was finally not going to be poor anymore. I knew my dream would be a success...which reminded me of money...which reminded me of bills. From there I segued from thoughts of prosperity into thinking instead of what bills had to be paid that day.

I opened my purse to get my checkbook and saw it was filled with shopping residue, a catchall of receipts and change all jumbled together. Extracting the checkbook caused this mass of papers and the balance of my paycheck in twenties, tens and singles to cascade into my purse and onto the floor. In the midst of getting annoyed at myself, I started laughing. Here I was thinking what I mess I had made by not being more orderly like you're supposed to be – putting money in a wallet, receipts neatly together – and yet creating this mess gave the appearance of being rich. Money was literally falling out of my checkbook, overflowing my purse. It really looked like I suddenly had a lot of money, a great deal more than I actually had. There was so much, it couldn't be contained. I was amazed at how wealthy I felt, all based on just an appearance, not reality. I really felt like I had an abundance of money.

We must be willing to get rid of the life we've planned,
So as to have the life that is waiting for us.
- Joseph Campbell

The more we allow ourselves to unfold,
the less likely we are to unravel.
- Rabbi Irwin Kula

Then I recalled what I had been thinking about just moments before: my business. I was constantly asking for signs that I was headed in the right direction, "show me the way to go home," confirmation my decision was right. Often I did get my signs at the most opportune moments, like when paying bills and feeling too poor to be able to cover them. Ask for signs. They will come. You just have to pay attention.

Write down what you want to experience. Spend time every day focusing on what you want to have, not on what you don't have. Let your actions be a reflection of your thoughts. Begin moving in the direction that you want to go, and your life will start to change.

Prepare for the event. Create a space for what you desire in your life. Imagine that it is yours already. Generate as much feeling as you can. Send that energy wave out to attract it. Then it must appear and it will.

At some point on our path of spiritual evolution, we hopefully find that the need for control diminishes and is replaced by a willingness to release our attachment to outcomes. We realize that there really is a purpose for us being here. We begin to say yes to an alignment with our inner calling, even if we don't know where that path is leading.

Believe. The process works. You supply the energy. Magic will happen.

Thought is the real causative force in life,
and there is no other. - Emmet Fox

We get in trouble not for what we don't
know, but for what we know and don't pay
attention to. - Alan Cohen

APPENDIX I: EXERCISES
CHAPTER 1

DESTINATION: SUCCESS

1. List some things in your life, that you are grateful for.
   "I am so thankful to have in my life:"
1.
2.
3.
4.
5.

2. List 3 things that are missing from your life, that you would like to have.
"I would feel successful in health, wealth, or happiness, if the following were part of my life:"

Goal #1:

Goal #2:

Goal #3:

3. Name one or more action steps necessary for each goal to manifest:

Goal #1:

Goal #2:

Goal #3:

> In oneself lies the whole world, and if you know how to look and learn, then the door is there and the key is in your hand.
> - J. Krishnamurti

The future belongs to those who believe in the beauty of their dreams.
- Eleanor Roosevelt

APPENDIX I: EXERCISES
CHAPTER 2

LIFE CHANGING EXPERIENCES

Think of two things you **Like** to do. Name it, WHAT it is. Describe in a few words the experience you had the first time you did it, or WHY you like it. Then show the RESULT, how it affected your life choices.

1. Something I like to do because I'm good at it:

The first time I did this it made me feel:

Because of my reaction, I ended up doing:

2. Something else I like to do for another reason:

The first time I did this it made me feel:

Because of my reaction, I made this life choice:

EXERCISES
CHAPTER 2 (cont'd)

LIFE CHANGING EXPERIENCES

Think of two things you **Do Not Like** to do. Name it, WHAT it is. Describe in a few words the experience you had the first time you did it, or WHY you did not like it. Then show the RESULT, how it affected your life choices.

1. An activity I do not like to do:

The first time I did this it made me feel:

Because of my reaction, I ended up doing:

2. Something else I prefer not to do for another reason:

The first time I did this it made me feel:

Because of my reaction, I made this life choice:

APPENDIX I: EXERCISES
CHAPTER 3

HEREDITY AND EXPERIENCES

1. Name something you or others find pleasing or displeasing about your appearance:

Describe how you think this affects how someone treats you:

To be treated differently, this would have to change:

2. Think of an event when you lost something of great value to you - a person, object, or job. What happened:

How you handled it. Your reaction:

Do you think this was the best choice? Something else you could have done:

3. Describe an action you thought would have a good outcome, but didn't:

The desired consequences of this action:

Actual Result:

Would you still choose the same action...Why:

Socrates, upon being told that he was the wisest man, said it was probably true, for he knew enough to know that he knew nothing. - Emma Curtis Hopkins

Three things cannot be long hidden:
the sun, the moon, and the truth.
- Buddha

APPENDIX I: EXERCISES
CHAPTER 4

THE POWER OF JUDGMENTS

1. Think of a negative experience that strongly affected you. Describe it and how it made you feel:

How could you think of this differently to remove its power over you:

2. State a prejudice that you learned from a family member or friend:

Have you ever questioned this or changed your position on this and why/why not:

Is this a biased or an informed judgment? Do you think this is justified or not and why:

3. Think of an event when a family member or friend criticized you and hurt your feelings. Fair or unfair. How did it affect you?

Did you let go of it or does it still affect you today and how:

Another way you could have reacted to the criticism:

The present is ours to enjoy, the future ours to create.
- Christian D. Larson

To improve our circumstances, we
must first increase our knowledge
and enlarge our consciousness.
- J.B. Goldstone

APPENDIX I: EXERCISES
CHAPTER 5

DOMINANT NEED

Describe an action, something you would like to do but you are not doing:

Why you are not doing this:

What you would have to change so that you could do it:

This choice is/is not possible...why:

What was your choice instead and why:

What information would you need to change that decision:

Then you would choose to do:

EXAMPLE:
I'd like to go to lunch.
Too early, too crowded.
Less people, faster service.
No
Wait
Knowledge that it wasn't crowded.
Leave now

What we expect, that we shall find.
- Plato

Problems must
inevitably arise, but
they can only be a
blessing because it is
through these problems
that we rise higher in
consciousness and
through that rising,
harmony is brought into
our daily life.
- Joel Goldsmith,
Practicing the Presence

APPENDIX I: EXERCISES
CHAPTER 6

FIND THE SILVER LINING

Think of three events in your life that you have judged to be negative. Write briefly the circumstances of each, followed by the possible lesson it was teaching you or other positive viewpoint that resulted from each instance.

Negative Event #1:

Silver Lining:

Negative Event #2:

Silver Lining:

Negative Event #3:

Silver Lining:

At the center of your being you have the answer.
You know who you are and you know what you want.
- Lao-tzu

Whatever you can do, or dream you
can, begin it. Boldness has genius,
power, and magic in it.
- Goethe

APPENDIX I: EXERCISES
CHAPTER 7

MONICA SCENARIO

Monica is washing dishes in the kitchen. Bob comes home and sees the dog in the backyard chasing a bag. Then he realizes there is garbage strewn all over the yard. He comes into the house fuming and yells to Monica.

"What are you doing? Aren't you keeping an eye on what's going on?
"What's going on?"
"The dog ripped open the garbage bag and there's a mess all over the yard and you're in here doing dishes! Is this how you take care of the house?"

Monica dries her hands and without a word goes out and starts to pick up the trash. A few minutes later Bob walks into the kitchen. Monica comes back into the house to the sound of cabinet doors being slammed.

"Isn't there a clean glass in this house? What have you been doing all day while I've been working?"
"Bob, what's wrong with you? What happened at work today?"
"Oh, the boss is having problems with his kids and then came down on me because I was late this morning. I had to stop and get gas. Someone didn't remember to fill the tank the last time they borrowed it."
"Talk to your son. It wasn't me this time."
"I already did that. I called him at lunchtime on his cell. He said it was full when he left it Saturday night. Wait. Didn't you take the car Sunday night for a meeting?"
"Oh, guess I did."
"And you couldn't take the time to fill it again when you know I have to go to work the next morning?"
"It was late. I was tired. I didn't even think to check the gas. I just wanted to get home."
"Well, thanks a lot. You probably just cost me my bonus this month!"
"Really, Bob. A few minutes is going to cost you your bonus? I don't think so."
"Oh, so now you're going to lay the blame on me? You're the one who couldn't take the time to fill the tank and I'm the one who has to pay for it! Am I the only one who is responsible in this house?"

ANALYSE Actions and Reactions:

Monica:

Bob:

Son:

Issues to consider: blame, responsibility for actions, wrong can't be undone, guilt, judgment, criticism, change of priorities or dominant need.

APPENDIX I: EXERCISES
CHAPTER 8

TRY HARDER

Think of a situation where you faulted yourself for not doing better. Describe it:

What would have to change for you to be able to do the job better:

Why you were not doing your best:

What your best would have looked like:

Why was it the only thing you could do at the time:

Go confidently in the direction of your dreams!
Live the life you've imagined. - Henry David Thoreau

Sometimes it takes a lifetime to
become clear. No matter, it may be
the most worthwhile way to spend
the time.
- Rachel Naomi Remen

APPENDIX I: EXERCISES
CHAPTER 9

CYA- CHANGE YOUR ATTITUDE

REPEAT THE FOLLOWING STATEMENTS.

THINK ABOUT WHAT YOU ARE SAYING AND WHAT IT MEANS.

1. _(Fill in problem)_ is a reality that either I do not have the power to change, or I am unwilling to pay the price to change.

2. No matter how much I wish things were otherwise, they are the way they are, and not the way I want them.

3. No matter how upsetting I find this, it is reality and I must accept that it is and just let it be.

4. The more emotional attachment I have to this, the more I give it power over me.

5. It is always _my choice_ to give away my power and let something outside myself determine whether or not I will be happy.

6. Every time I give my power away, I undermine my own self esteem.

7. Therefore I choose to take care of myself and let this be.

8. I choose to not let this have a negative effect on me.

It is the light of the mind which determines
whether you see confusion and limitation or
whether you see order and abundance.
- Ervin Seale

Happiness is the consequence
of personal effort. You have
to participate relentlessly in
the manifestation of your
own blessings.
- Elizabeth Gilbert

APPENDIX I: EXERCISES
CHAPTER 10

CHOICE

Name something in your life situation you would like to do that you are not now doing:

Why you aren't doing it:

Is it possible for you to change this condition so you are able to do the desired action and what that change would be:

Is this acceptable or is the price you must pay too high to change:

Any other reasons for not doing it:

Steps necessary for change :

The scattered inner life, as a rule, is put together by picking up the scattered pieces and setting them in place... - Frederick W. Bailes

When I dare to be powerful – to use my strength in the service of my vision, then it becomes less and less important whether I am afraid. - Audre Lorde

APPENDIX I: EXERCISES
CHAPTER 11

FAILURE

Write about your worst failure:

Write about the good, or imagined good, that came from it:

Now you know that the worst can happen to you and you will survive it !

Water gives life to ten thousand things
and does not strive. - Lao Tzu

The only decision we need
to make is to begin.
- Eric Butterworth

APPENDIX I: EXERCISES
CHAPTER 12

GET OVER IT

Recall an experience of losing something that still bothers you. Describe:

Why you can't let it go:

What good you feel you are getting by holding on to this negative experience:

Is it worth the price you are paying...And Why:

A positive action you can do to solve it:

Then Do it or get over it.

You have to go past the turbulence of internal dialogue to connect with that abundant, affluent, infinite, creative mind. - Deepak Chopra

The whole of truth
is always here, open
to us; however, it is
necessary that we
find it for
ourselves.
- Nona L. Brooks

APPENDIX I: EXERCISES
CHAPTER 13

THE LESSON

Choose a negative experience that had serious or important consequences for you.
What happened:

What was the Lesson:

Did you GET the lesson or will it repeat itself...Why:

Do you think you will GET it next time...Why:

Take the first step in faith. You don't have to see the whole staircase, just take the first step.

- Martin Luther King, Jr.

It doesn't matter how long we have had a negative pattern. The point of power is in the present moment. - Louise Hay

APPENDIX I: EXERCISES
CHAPTER 14

HOW TO

STOP THE RIPPLE EFFECT

Whenever you find yourself feeling bad, down, depressed because nothing seems to be going right, use this method to turn your thinking and attitude around to the positive.

1. As soon as you find yourself thinking negative thoughts, one followed by another, and another— STOP your thought process.

2. Take control of your thoughts and think of just one positive thing, one good experience that has happened at any time in your life. Doesn't matter how small or what it was.

3. Hold that thought. Remember it in detail. Recall how good it made you feel.

4. Realize that because this one thing happened, it is therefore possible to have more positive events in your experience. It has happened to you already.

5. Think of one more positive event.

6. Remember another.

7. Continue this process until you can say and believe the following:
   If it has happened before - and it has - it can happen again. Positive things do happen
   in my life.

8. Repeat it as many times as necessary. Believe it.

A great tool to use during this ritual is your Gratitude Rock. Hold it in your hand, rub it, toss it, while you go through the process.

> Never take less than the very best that can be had at the present time; but do not waste energy by desiring what cannot be had at the present time.
> - Wallace D. Wattles

> Happiness is something that you are, and it comes from the way you think.
> -Wayne Dyer

APPENDIX I: EXERCISES
CHAPTER 15

EXPECTATIONS

1. Think about someone you like who you feel has failed you, disappointed you. Describe the action the person did:

What were your expectations that were not fulfilled? What you think the person should have done:

What was the consequence of this action:

Is there another way you can look at this to make it okay again:

2. Think of someone who made you angry. Why:

Are you making it personal...Why:

What the payoff is for holding on to this feeling:

What happens if you let it go:

> In my end is my beginning.
> - T.S. Eliot

> Everything can be taken from a man but one thing: the last of human freedoms – to choose one's attitude in any given set of circumstances, to choose one's own way.
> - Viktor Frankl

APPENDIX I: EXERCISES
CHAPTER 16

THE LAST EXERCISE

How to deal with a traumatic event

Think of an experience that is or was difficult to handle because of the loss of a loved one, a job, an opportunity. Something that devastated you. Describe it in a few words:

As this is in the past, think of what possible good came from this later. If a loved one, then think of the memories. If a job, then the good you experienced with it. If a lost opportunity, then what new door opened for you instead. Describe:

Now let the pain go and entertain yourself with something new or something of interest to you. What could that be:

Certain things catch our eye. But pursue only
those things that capture your heart.
- Native American saying

Sunrise, sunset.

APPENDIX II

FOOD FOR THOUGHT

"Even if you're on the right track, you'll get run over if you just sit there."
- Will Rogers

"This is the true joy in life: the being used for a purpose recognized by yourself as a mighty one; the being a force of nature instead of a feverish, selfish little clod of ailments and grievances complaining that the world will not devote itself to making you happy. I am of the opinion that my life belongs to the whole community, and as long as I live, it is my privilege to do for it whatever I can. I want to be thoroughly used up when I die, for the harder I work the more I live. I rejoice in life for its own sake. Life is no 'brief candle' to me. It is a sort of splendid torch which I have got hold of for the moment, and I want to make it burn as brightly as possible before handing it on to future generations."
- George Bernard Shaw

"We who lived in concentration camps can remember the men who walked through the huts comforting others, giving away their last piece of bread. They may have been few in number, but they offer sufficient proof that everything can be taken from a man but one thing: the last of the human freedoms - to choose one's attitude in any given set of circumstances."
- Victor Frankl

"Agreement doesn't spring to mind as the primary way to handle our adversaries because, of course, we're right and they're not. It's true that agreeing with them shortens the conversation and conserves our energy. This is all assuming our adversaries are other people. But most adversarial energy is around our own collective thinking."
- Jessie Jennings

"Bless me Spirit this day, and may my life be a blessing to others."
- L.M. Gacher

"You are a spiritual being embodying all of the Power of the Universe within you. Will you not accept the Truth and start living as the Light of the world that you are?"
- John Randolph Price

"Every time you actualize more of your potential by becoming more yourself, your joy increases, regardless of what's going on in your external circumstances."
- Rev. Dr. Michael Beckwith

Each of us has an ego. That part of us that says "I am".
A healthy ego recognizes the value of yourself, who you are, and knows that everyone is of equal value. It allows you to stand up for yourself without pushing anyone else around.
A Big ego places a higher value on themselves, and a Small ego feels not worthy.

"Be blessed by day. Be blessed by night. Stay safe in spirit, love, and light."
L.M. Gacher

To become different from what we are,
we must have some awareness
of what we are.
- Eric Hoffer

Rise & Shine

A Conscious Way of Life

Tools to Meet the Challenges of Life Series

Rise&Shine was written from life experience when I was beyond miserable, and then saw my last dream shattered. Every morning I still woke up, forced to face another day. I slowly realized I had to find a solution. I could not change anything that had happened. The only thing that was within my power to change was my attitude. I had to find another way to look at life. The result you hold in your hands. This book is transformational. Every time I read it, it changes me again. It can do the same for you. Set you on the right path. Straighten things out. Make it easier to understand why things happen and how to handle it all. Everyone has problems and issues in life. In the end, we are not all so different. You do have the power to change your life. You must believe in yourself first. All else follows. Choose to live a conscious life: awake, aware, responsible. This book will give you the tools, show you how to meet the challenges of life. Erase all doubt. You can do it.

We use about 10% of what we read. That number goes up to 18% when we add a home study course to the equation. However, the number goes way up to 89% when we add a mentor or coach to our program of success. Both of these choices are available to you.

So if you read and study this on your own, be sure to do the exercises in Appendix I for each chapter. They are designed to help you apply the principles to your life. Use the bold text to quickly scan the ideas presented in each chapter.

When you enroll in the six week online home study course, it includes interactive forums, and two bonus live webinars with one-on-one active participation with this author. Enroll with a group of friends and you will have the ability to participate together in the forums and webinars. You can find more information at www.highesteemseminars.com.

You may schedule a personal counseling session at www.toughluvcounseling.com. As a Certified Professional Life Coach, I practice a unique combination of intuitive personal counseling with life coaching, in an atmosphere of tough love. You will find it to be a most refreshing, practical, logical and down-to-earth experience. To see how it will benefit you, schedule a free 20 minute consultation.

You may reach this author online at loismarieg@highesteemseminars.com or call toll free at 888-834-0514.

Lois Marie Gacher
PO Box 133
San Jose, NM 87565-0133

We are all capable of much
more than we think we are.
- Lao Tzu

And so... life goes on.
- Irv Kupcinet